100% Curriculum Vocabulary

Lynn Eggleston
Laura Larson

Skill Area:	Vocabulary
Ages:	11 through 18
Grades:	6 through 12

LinguiSystems

LinguiSystems, Inc.
3100 4th Avenue
East Moline, IL 61244-9700
1-800 PRO IDEA
1-800-776-4332

FAX: 1-800-577-4555
E-mail: service@linguisystems.com
Web: www.linguisystems.com
TDD: 1-800-933-8331
(for those with hearing impairments)

Copyright © 2002 LinguiSystems, Inc.

All of our products are copyrighted to protect the fine work of our authors. Copying this entire book for any reason is prohibited. You may, however, copy the worksheets as needed for your own use with students.

Any other reproduction or distribution of these worksheets is not allowed, including copying this book to use as another primary source or "master" copy.

Printed in the U.S.A.
ISBN 0-7606-0422-3

About the Authors

Lynn Eggleston, **M.S., CCC-SLP**, has over 20 years of experience as a speech-language pathologist and ESL teacher. She has worked in a variety of settings including schools (preschool–12), hospitals, rehabilitation centers, and subacute and long-term care facilities. Currently, Lynn lives in Mesa, AZ, where she is a speech-language pathologist for the Phoenix Union High School District. Lynn works with developmentally delayed students with a variety of special needs in the areas of phonology, language, articulation, fluency, voice, and pragmatic impairments. In her spare time, Lynn enjoys traveling, hiking, swimming, reading, and writing. This is Lynn's first publication with LinguiSystems.

Laura Larson, **M.S. CCC-SLP**, has been working with developmentally delayed, TBI, ESL and LD high school students in the Phoenix Union High School District since 1998. Laura has also provided therapy services for adult patients in subacute and long-term care facilities, as well as therapy for home health care patients. Currently, Laura resides in Mesa, AZ, with her husband and enjoys swimming, hiking, reading, and traveling in her spare time. This is Laura's first publication with LinguiSystems.

Acknowledgments

A special thanks to Brook Larson for all of his hard work on the book. We also want to thank our students at Alhambra, Maryvale, and South Mountain High Schools for allowing us to try out and develop this book.

We dedicate *100% Curriculum Vocabulary* to our families.

Edited by Denise L. Kelly & Lauri Whiskeyman
Page Layout by Denise L. Kelly & Christine Buysse

Table of Contents

Introduction 5

Vocabulary Lists 8

Art 1 19
Art 2 25

Biology 1 31
Biology 2 37
Biology 3 43
Biology 4 49
Biology 5 55

Consumer 1 61
Consumer 2 67
Consumer 3 73
Consumer 4 79

Earth Science 1 85
Earth Science 2 91
Earth Science 3 97
Earth Science 4 103
Earth Science 5 109
Earth Science 6 115
Earth Science 7 121

English 1 127
English 2 133
English 3 139
English 4 145
English 5 151
English 6 157
English 7 163

Table of Contents, continued

Government 1 169
Government 2 175
Government 3 181

Health 1 187
Health 2 193
Health 3 199
Health 4 205
Health 5 211

History 1 217
History 2 223
History 3 229

Keyboarding 1 235
Keyboarding 2 241
Keyboarding 3 247

Math 1 253
Math 2 259
Math 3 265
Math 4 271

Answer Key 277

Introduction

The current Individuals with Disabilities Education Act (IDEA) promotes the idea that resource specialists and therapists must provide services that are educationally relevant and aligned with each school's curriculum. Many states also require students to pass state exams in order to receive a diploma. In addition, many school districts are placing special education students into regular classrooms. The challenge for therapists and resource specialists is to make school assignments and therapy activities relevant and meaningful for the students by relating them to classroom content areas.

As speech-language pathologists working in the public schools, we have found a lack of curriculum-related resources for junior and senior high school students. We have also found that many of our language-disordered and ESL students experience difficulties understanding and learning classroom vocabulary. These students require repetition and a variety of exercises in order to learn information. Frequently, resource specialists and therapists have many demands on their time and are unable to consult and collaborate with each student's teachers in order to incorporate classroom information into therapy or activities. We created *100% Curriculum Vocabulary* to provide relevant, core-curriculum vocabulary practice. This book will not only enable you to help students increase their vocabulary, semantics, syntax, reading, and writing skills, but it will help them do better in their core English, Science, and Math classes, and on school achievement tests.

100% Curriculum Vocabulary has been used with regular education students and students who have learning disabilities, emotional handicaps, mild mental retardation, and limited English proficiency. The repetition and the variety of the activities will help students learn and remember the core vocabulary words. We realize that the curriculum in different schools teaches different vocabulary, but we feel the vocabulary in this book is important for all students to learn.

Each section contains definitions, fill-in-the-blanks, word associations, writing sentences, crossword puzzles, and word searches. These activities can be done with individual students, small groups, or entire classrooms. The activities also provide functional material that students can read aloud to practice articulation, develop fluency skills, or remediate voice difficulties. In addition, the activities are great practice for students who have problems with reading or writing skills. Most importantly, the relevant vocabulary motivates students to work on materials that will help improve their grades in classroom subjects.

Introduction, continued

How to Use This Book
Begin by examining each student's class schedule to find out which classes or subjects the student is currently enrolled in. The worksheets from *100% Curriculum Vocabulary* should be used as support materials for these classes. Choose applicable sections from this book and work through them. Each section is described below.

- *Definitions*
  Have the student read each word aloud and ask him to provide a definition. If the student is unable to give a definition, have him read the definition provided. Next, try to get the student to relate the word to his prior knowledge. If he is unable to do this, try to relate the word to something familiar to the student. Finally, see if the student can explain what each word means in his own words.

- *Fill-in-the-Blank*
  Challenge the student to complete this activity without referring to the Definitions page. After the student has completed all of the items he can, allow him to use the Definitions page to complete the remaining items.

- *Word Association*
  Again, have the student attempt this activity without referring to the Definitions page. If the student needs help, provide cues by referring to the student's prior knowledge or his own definitions. After providing cues, allow the student to use the Definitions page to complete the remaining items.

- *Writing Sentences*
  Encourage the student to write a sentence using each word without referring to the Definitions page and to use the word in a familiar context.

- *Crossword Puzzle & Word Search*
  The pages are provided as extra practice activities. The crosswords do not have the vocabulary words listed. If the student is having trouble remembering the vocabulary words, allow him to use the Word Search list of words. If the student still has difficulty completing the puzzle, allow him to refer to the Definitions page. When completing the word search pages, have the student try to find each word in the puzzle. After the student finds the word, have him explain what the word means. You can also assign these activities for homework so the student can practice the vocabulary at home.

Introduction, continued

Extra Practice
These tips will help you use the activities in this book to support ongoing speech and language goals:

✔ Underline the targeted phoneme on each page to help students with articulation errors. Then, have them read aloud as they complete the activities. Encourage them to self-monitor their production.

✔ Have students practice their fluency-shaping strategies while reading aloud or discussing vocabulary words.

✔ Tape-record or videotape students as they read aloud and/or speak to help them self-monitor fluency strategies and their use of secondary behaviors.

✔ Encourage voice students to work on vocal strategies, such as relaxation, vocal inflection, pitch, and stress while reading the activities aloud.

The overall goal of the activities in *100% Curriculum Vocabulary* is to provide students with accessible ways to approach and use the vocabulary they encounter in the classroom. If they are able to master these words and their uses, they are well on their way to becoming more motivated, successful students. They will do better on their daily assignments and on tests, and will feel a greater sense of achievement. Teachers will appreciate the support for the curriculum the activities in this book provide. Students will appreciate the extra help they receive and will be more likely to be involved and on task in their classrooms.

Lynn & Laura

Vocabulary List — Art

Art 1

abstract
balanced
bright
calligraphy
casting
collage
contour
contrast
design
glaze

Art 2

ceramics
hue
illusion
kiln
line
pattern
perspective
pigment
primary color
texture

Vocabulary List — Biology

Biology 1

aorta
colon
cornea
esophagus
gall gladder
kidneys
lungs
lymph nodes
organ
small intestine

Biology 2

chromosomes
clone
dominant trait
gene
heredity
meiosis
mitosis
mutation
recessive trait
traits

Biology 3

alveoli
antibiotics
antibody
antigen
artery
bacteria
capillary
clot
immunity
marrow

Biology 4

carnivore
consumer
decomposer
food chain
herbivore
invertebrate
organism
parasite
producer
venom

Biology 5

anterior
cartilage
central nervous system
disease
element
embryo
joint
molecule
posterior
virus

Vocabulary List — Consumer

Consumer 1

adjust
balance
biweekly
checking account
expenditure
gross pay
interest
net pay
salary
withhold

Consumer 2

address
application
company
employee
interview
position
promotion
résumé
schedule
time card

Consumer 3

advertisement
credit card
discount
identification
lease
mean
mortgage
odds
rent
sale price

Consumer 4

car pool
detour
lane
merge
pedestrian
prohibited
residential
restriction
shoulder
visibility

Vocabulary List: Earth Science

Earth Science 1

atmosphere
barometer
Celsius
climate
evaporation
Fahrenheit
hurricane
precipitation
saturated
tornado

Earth Science 2

asteroid
astronomer
black hole
constellation
galaxy
meteor
nebula
orbit
planet
supernova

Earth Science 3

anther
deciduous
fruit
photosynthesis
pistil
pollen
roots
seed
stamen
stem

Earth Science 4

acid rain
alluvial fan
catalytic converter
cavern
crest
delta
desalination
erosion
irrigation
pollutant

Earth Science 5

Big Bang theory
Cenozoic era
earthquake
epicenter
glacier
iceberg
igneous rock
Mesozoic era
Paleozoic era
Precambrian era

Earth Science 6

alloy
conservation
contract
core
data
depletion
element
expand
fossil
fossil fuel

Earth Science 7

adaptation
condensation
conduction
conifer
elevation
equator
front
hazardous waste
hemisphere
quasar

Vocabulary List — English

English 1

abbreviation
apostrophe
capitalize
colon
comma
contraction
end marks
proofread
quotation marks
semicolon

English 2

adjective
adverb
comparative
metaphor
noun
pronoun
proper noun
simile
superlative
verb

English 3

conclusion
context
diagram
draft
idea
main idea
order
paragraph
plagiarism
topic

English 4

analogy
anecdote
anonymous
author
character
idiom
myth
nonfiction
persuasion
plot

English 5

accept
among
between
clarify
except
explanation
fact
instruction
mediate
opinion

English 6

dictionary
principal
principle
than
their
then
there
they're
you're
your

English 7

autobiography
clause
dependent clause (subordinate)
description
detail
double negative
encyclopedia
independent clause (main)
phrase
statement

Vocabulary List: Government

Government 1

boycott
deficit
document
economy
excise tax
free enterprise
loss
profit
surplus
tariff

Government 2

Congress
consent
democracy
executive branch
House of Representatives
judicial system
monarchy
Senate
session
veto

Government 3

acquit
candidate
debate
immigrant
indict
jury
majority
minority
native
voter

Vocabulary List — Health

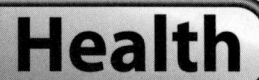

Health 1

abuse
body language
denial
displacement
emotion
extrovert
introvert
neglect
personality
risk behavior

Health 2

emphysema
high blood pressure
homeostasis
quality of life
sleep apnea
stress
stroke
ulcer
values
wellness

Health 3

adrenaline
carbohydrates
carcinogen
dehydration
digestion
habit
immune system
metabolism
narcotic
physical environment

Health 4

asthma
astigmatism
color blindness
diaphragm
epilepsy
Eustachian tube
Fetal Alcohol Syndrome
gingivitis
plaque
vaccination

Health 5

amnesia
anorexia nervosa
anxiety disorder
bulimia
depression
manic-depressive disorder
obsessive-compulsive disorder
phobia
psychiatrist
schizophrenia

Vocabulary List — History

History 1

abolitionist
blockade
carpetbaggers
Confederacy
indentured servants
plantation
secede
sharecropping
Underground Railroad
Union

History 2

anti-Semitism
concentration camp
dictator
emigrate
Holocaust
invasion
overthrow
ration
refugees
traitor

History 3

boycott
colonies
depression
Dust Bowl
expansion
forty-niners
loyalists
Prohibition
truce
wagon train

Vocabulary List — Keyboarding

Keyboarding 1

Backspace
Caps Lock
Control
Enter
Escape
Insert
keyboard
Shift
Tab
word processing

Keyboarding 2

accuracy
delete
directory
error
indent
print
retrieve
save
search
word wrap

Keyboarding 3

backup copy
bold
centering
cursor
double space
format
header/footer
margin
printer
single space

Vocabulary List — Math

Math 1

angle
arc
bisect
circumference
congruent
diameter
geometry
parallel lines
perimeter
tangent

Math 2

compass
decrease
denominator
dividend
division
fraction
increase
numerator
percent
protractor

Math 3

addition
algebra
bar graph
coordinates
decimal
equation
even number
integer
line graph
negative number

Math 4

foot
gallon
inch
length
pound
quart
review
solution
volume
yard

1 Definitions — Art

1. **abstract** — a picture that does not look real

2. **balanced** — a work of art that is equal in weight and color

3. **bright** — very clear and light

4. **calligraphy** — decorative, elegant handwriting

5. **casting** — to make or form something by pouring a liquid or soft material into a mold and letting it harden

6. **collage** — a picture made by pasting pictures, objects, or newspaper to a surface

7. **contour** — the outline or shape of a figure

8. **contrast** — the amount of difference between the lightest and darkest parts in a work of art

9. **design** — to make a drawing

10. **glaze** — a thin, clear coating spread over a painted surface to make it shiny

2 Fill-in-the-Blank   Art

Fill in the blanks with the words from the box.

| abstract | bright | casting | contour | design |
| balanced | calligraphy | collage | contrast | glaze |

1. The amount of difference between the lightest and darkest parts in a work of art is the _____.

2. Decorative, elegant handwriting is _____.

3. To _____ is to make a drawing.

4. An _____ picture does not look real.

5. To make a shiny surface, a person uses _____.

6. A _____ work of art has equal amounts of weight and color.

7. Yellow is a _____ color.

8. The outline of a figure is a _____.

9. A _____ is a picture made by pasting items to a surface.

10. _____ is making something by pouring a liquid into a mold and letting it harden.

1 Word Association — Art

Write the word from the box next to the word or phrase that shares a similar meaning.

| abstract | bright | casting | contour | design |
| balanced | calligraphy | collage | contrast | glaze |

1. clear and light   _____

2. make a drawing   _____

3. has equal parts   _____

4. amount of difference   _____

5. handwriting   _____

6. not real   _____

7. coating   _____

8. outline   _____

9. mold   _____

10. pasting objects to a surface _____

1 Writing Sentences — Art

Write a sentence using each word.

1. abstract

2. balance

3. bright

4. calligraphy

5. casting

6. collage

7. contour

8. contrast

9. design

10. glaze

Crossword Puzzle — Art

Complete the puzzle with words that match the clues.

Across

1. decorative, elegant handwriting
4. the outline or shape of a figure
5. a work of art that is equal in weight and color
7. to make or form something by pouring a liquid or soft material into a mold and letting it harden
9. a picture made by pasting pictures, objects, or newspaper to a surface

Down

2. a picture that does not look real
3. very clear and light
4. the amount of difference between the lightest and darkest parts in a work of art
6. to make a drawing
8. a thin, clear coating spread over a painted surface to make it shiny

1 Word Search — Art

All of the words listed in the box appear in the puzzle — horizontally, vertically, diagonally, or backward. Find and circle them.

abstract	bright	casting	contour	design
balanced	calligraphy	collage	contrast	glaze

```
B W Q N V S C Q D E G U I J V
Q R O U O N A T G S G W A K W
A Q I K M L L A S U T G C V C
B X O G Q G L C U A L U M L C
G G E Q H L I B A A R K K L B
N T H J O T G X Z X D T E X P
I Y W C S Z R E T T E G N B R
T A U S F Z A F S M S P M O A
S X H I Z O P A F K I G I B C
A F R S M U H I Y N G R S W W
C C A T X I Y R C O N T O U R
D E C N A L A B D X R U U K N
D R M K M V R D O A F U Z Q B
E J C J M Z X G C G U P D Y U
K K J I R C Y T N K F T X H W
```

100% Curriculum Vocabulary—Grades 6-12   24   Copyright © 2002 LinguiSystems, Inc.

② Definitions — Art

1. **ceramics** — the art of shaping pottery from clay and then baking it

2. **hue** — one shade of a color

3. **illusion** — something that looks real, but is fake

4. **kiln** — an oven used to bake clay into ceramics

5. **line** — a continuous mark made by a pen, pencil, brush, or other tool

6. **pattern** — a design that is repeated

7. **perspective** — an art technique used to represent distances or items that are near and far in a painting or drawing

8. **pigment** — a mineral or dye that is mixed with oil or water to make color in paint

9. **primary color** — a color (red, yellow, or blue) that can be mixed with another color to make all other colors

10. **texture** — the feel of the surface of an object (bumpy, smooth, etc.)

100% Curriculum Vocabulary—Grades 6-12

2 Fill-in-the-Blank — Art

Fill in the blanks with the words or phrases from the box.

| illusion | pigment | kiln | primary color | pattern |
| perspective | line | texture | hue | ceramics |

1. Red _____ is used to dye a shirt red.

2. A _____ is one shade of a color.

3. A magician can perform an _____.

4. A _____ is a continuous mark made with a pen or pencil.

5. The art of making objects from clay is called _____.

6. You can create a _____ using stripes or plaids.

7. A bumpy surface has _____.

8. An example of a _____ is blue.

9. Clay is baked in a _____.

10. _____ is an art technique used to represent distances or items that are near and far in a painting or drawing.

2 Word Association — Art

Write the word or phrase from the box next to the word or phrase that shares a similar meaning.

> illusion   pigment   kiln   primary color   pattern
> perspective   line   texture   hue   ceramics

1. repetition _____
2. yellow, red, or blue _____
3. dye _____
4. not real _____
5. continuous mark _____
6. oven _____
7. feel of the surface _____
8. pottery _____
9. shade _____
10. represents distances _____

② Writing Sentences — Art

Write a sentence using each word or phrase.

1. ceramics _____
   _____

2. hue _____
   _____

3. illusion _____
   _____

4. kiln _____
   _____

5. line _____
   _____

6. pattern _____
   _____

7. perspective _____
   _____

8. pigment _____
   _____

9. primary color _____
   _____

10. texture _____
    _____

100% Curriculum Vocabulary—Grades 6-12

Crossword Puzzle — Art

Complete the puzzle with words that match the clues.

Across

1. a mineral or dye that is mixed with oil or water to make color in paint
5. an oven used to bake clay into ceramics
7. the feel of the surface of an object
8. one shade of a color
9. a color that can be mixed together with another to make all other colors

Down

1. an art technique used to represent distances or items that are near and far in a painting or drawing
2. a design that is repeated
3. a continuous mark made by a pen, pencil, or brush
4. the art of creating pottery that is made from clay and then baked
6. something that looks real, but is fake

② Word Search — Art

All the words or phrases listed in the box appear in the puzzle — horizontally, vertically, diagonally, or backward. Find and circle them.

illusion	pigment	kiln	primary color	pattern
perspective	line	texture	hue	ceramics

```
E R Z C D Q C F P K V R C U N
K R O X U H P E F I O Q Q U I
W M U Q D A Z X R L J K I R L
X J Q T T J D C O A E V F Z L
U E Y T X S B C C N M E B D U
X Y E N Q E Y U I J I I K G S
S R H U E R T L C S S S C I I
N N E A A P G L Z N P N Q S O
J T X M A R S T R J X S N K N
O E I I R W T Z H F H D L A Y
R R G V G T N E M G I P I M R
P E R S P E C T I V E H K M W
```

Definitions — Biology

1. **aorta** — the largest blood vessel in the body

2. **colon** — the lower part of the large intestine that absorbs water and makes waste

3. **cornea** — the clear, outer layer of the eye that lets in light

4. **esophagus** — a tube that pushes food to the stomach

5. **gall bladder** — a small sac that is attached to the liver and stores bile (liquid that helps digest fats) until it is needed

6. **kidneys** — two bean-shaped organs that take liquid waste from the blood and turn it into urine

7. **lungs** — a pair of sac-like organs in the chest that put oxygen into the blood

8. **lymph nodes** — small oval capsules all over the body that destroy bacteria

9. **organ** — a group of tissues that work together to do a certain function, such as eyes for sight or lungs for breathing

10. **small intestine** — the long, tube-like organ where food is digested

1 Fill-in-the-Blank — Biology

Fill in the blanks with the words or phrases from the box.

| aorta | cornea | gall bladder | lungs | organ |
| colon | esophagus | kidneys | lymph nodes | small intestine |

1. _____ are small oval capsules all over the body that destroy bacteria.

2. The clear, outer layer of the eye that lets in light is the _____.

3. The _____ is the largest blood vessel in the body.

4. A person's _____ take liquid waste from the blood and turn it into urine.

5. To breathe air, a person needs to use his _____.

6. The _____ is the lower part of the large intestine that makes waste.

7. The small sac that is attached to the liver and stores bile is the _____.

8. The _____ is a tube that pushes food to the stomach.

9. A group of tissues that work together to do a certain function is an _____.

10. The long, tube-like organ where food is digested is the _____.

1. Word Association — Biology

Write the word or phrase from the box next to the word or phrase that shares a similar meaning.

aorta	cornea	gall bladder	lungs	organ
colon	esophagus	kidneys	lymph nodes	small intestine

1. tube-like organ _____

2. tissues that work together _____

3. sac-like organs _____

4. destroy bacteria _____

5. eye _____

6. stores bile _____

7. lower part of large intestine _____

8. pushes food to the stomach _____

9. turns waste into urine _____

10. largest blood vessel _____

① Writing Sentences — Biology

Write a sentence using each word or phrase.

1. aorta

2. colon

3. cornea

4. esophagus

5. gall bladder

6. kidneys

7. lungs

8. lymph nodes

9. organ

10. small intestine

Crossword Puzzle — Biology

Complete the puzzle with words that match the clues.

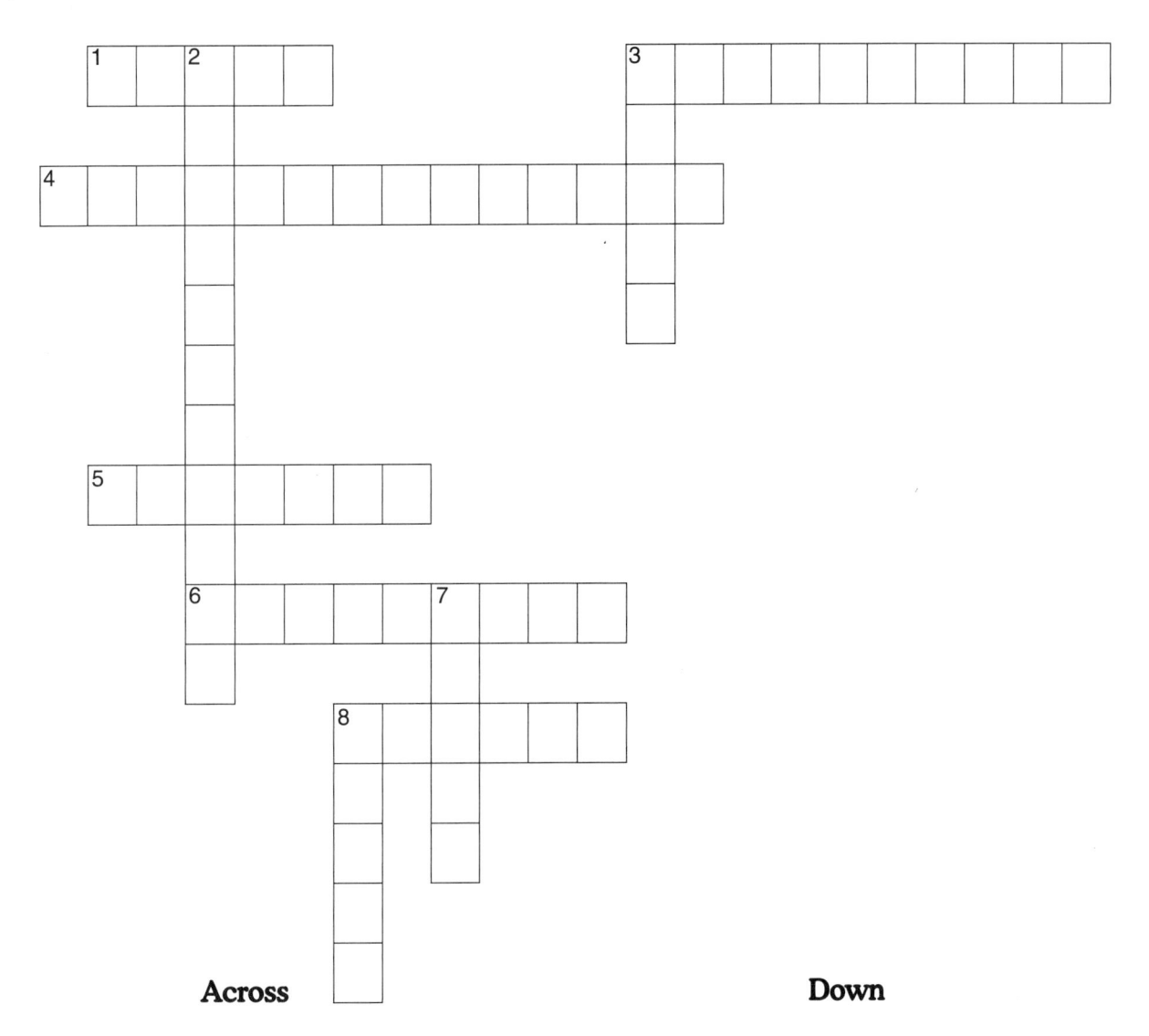

Across

1. a group of tissues that work together to do a certain function
3. small oval capsules all over the body that destroy bacteria
4. the long, tube-like organ where food is digested
5. two bean-shaped organs that take liquid waste from the blood and turn it into urine
6. a tube that pushes food to the stomach
8. the clear, outer layer of the eye that lets in light

Down

2. a small sac that is attached to the liver and stores bile until it is needed
3. a par of sac-like organs in the chest that put oxygen into the blood
7. the largest blood vessel in the body
8. the lower part of the large intestine that absorbs water and makes waste

100% Curriculum Vocabulary—Grades 6-12

1 Word Search

Biology

All the words or phrases listed in the box appear in the puzzle — horizontally, vertically, diagonally, or backward. Find and circle them.

| aorta | cornea | gall bladder | lungs | organ |
| colon | esophagus | kidneys | lymph nodes | small intestine |

```
S  U  G  A  H  P  O  S  E  L  A  G  F  J  E
D  M  T  S  M  L  U  V  Y  K  E  A  T  N  D
E  J  A  Z  Y  A  U  M  Z  B  N  L  C  O  X
S  B  Z  L  A  E  P  N  L  T  R  L  L  I  P
G  L  Z  B  L  H  N  N  G  U  O  B  G  R  D
O  R  G  A  N  I  O  D  R  S  C  L  S  H  F
Q  I  C  O  B  L  N  O  I  K  R  A  D  C  Q
O  G  D  Z  O  A  U  T  U  K  J  D  D  X  B
Z  E  I  C  J  O  S  H  E  C  N  D  I  V  S
S  I  I  L  P  R  C  T  L  S  A  E  A  R  D
W  X  X  R  P  T  Y  N  B  Z  T  R  I  A  V
H  T  U  T  Z  A  P  U  B  E  X  I  L  R  Y
C  R  V  K  J  J  V  I  W  A  H  W  N  V  R
F  P  B  X  X  T  M  J  K  R  L  J  Y  E  U
L  U  Y  J  A  D  W  A  C  B  W  A  J  W  Y
```

100% Curriculum Vocabulary—Grades 6-12   36   Copyright © 2002 LinguiSystems, Inc.

Definitions — Biology

1. **chromosomes** — structures in the center of a cell that carry genes

2. **clone** — an identical copy of something grown from a single cell of its parent

3. **dominant trait** — a trait that is visible or rules over other traits

4. **gene** — a tiny part of a chromosome that contains genetic information and controls traits

5. **heredity** — traits passed down from parents to children through genes

6. **meiosis** — a process that causes a cell to divide its chromosomes to become four new cells

7. **mitosis** — a process that causes a cell to divide its chromosomes to become two new cells

8. **mutation** — a change within a gene or chromosome resulting in a new feature

9. **recessive trait** — a trait that is hidden

10. **traits** — specific inherited characteristics such as eye or hair color that a person gets from his/her parents

2 Fill-in-the-Blank — Biology

Fill in the blanks with the words or phrases from the box.

| clone | dominant trait | chromosomes | recessive trait | mitosis |
| gene | mutation | traits | heredity | meiosis |

1. A trait that is hidden is a _____.

2. A change in a gene that results in a new feature is a _____.

3. A _____ is a tiny part of a chromosome that contains genetic information and controls traits.

4. Structures that carry genes are _____.

5. A _____ is visible or rules over other traits.

6. _____ is a process that causes a cell to divide its chromosomes to become two new cells.

7. An identical copy of something grown from a single cell of its parent is a _____.

8. Characteristics that a person gets from his/her parents are _____.

9. _____ is a process that causes a cell to divide its chromosomes to become four new cells.

10. Traits passed down from parents to children through genes is _____.

2 Word Association — Biology

Write the word or phrase from the box next to the word or phrase that shares a similar meaning.

| clone | dominant trait | chromosomes | recessive trait | mitosis |
| gene | mutation | traits | heredity | meiosis |

1. carries genes　　　　　　　　　_____

2. two new cells　　　　　　　　　_____

3. rules over other traits　　　　　_____

4. traits passed to children　　　　_____

5. change resulting in new feature　_____

6. four new cells　　　　　　　　　_____

7. hidden trait　　　　　　　　　　_____

8. identical copy　　　　　　　　　_____

9. controls traits　　　　　　　　　_____

10. brown hair and eyes　　　　　　_____

100% Curriculum Vocabulary—Grades 6-12　　　　Copyright © 2002 LinguiSystems, Inc.

② Writing Sentences — Biology

Write a sentence using each word or phrase.

1. chromosomes

2. clone

3. dominant trait

4. gene

5. heredity

6. meiosis

7. mitosis

8. mutation

9. recessive trait

10. traits

Crossword Puzzle 2 — Biology

Complete the puzzle with words that match the clues.

Across

3. a process that causes a cell to divide its chromosomes to become two new cells
5. traits passed down from parents to children through genes
6. a tiny part of a chromosome that contains genetic information and controls traits
10. a trait that is hidden

Down

1. characteristics that a person gets from his/her parents, such as eye or hair color
2. a trait that is visible or rules over other traits
4. structures in the center of a cell that carry genes
7. a change within a gene or chromosome resulting in a new feature
8. a process that causes a cell to divide its chromosomes to become four new cells
9. an identical copy of something grown from a single cell of its parent

② Word Search — Biology

All the words or phrases listed in the box appear in the puzzle — horizontally, vertically, diagonally, or backward. Find and circle them.

clone	dominant trait	chromosomes	recessive trait	mitosis
gene	mutation	traits	heredity	meiosis

```
Z B W T U T Z F I P H C T T M
O Z O S G E N E Y E M C I E U
C D O M I N A N T T R A I T T
F H Q F W S I B H G R U I S A
Z E R F T E O E A T J Y U T T
F B K O N F R T E U U Y R I I
M V V O M E E V I V U H U A O
Y O L W D O I X O M H X D R N
D C B I L S S I S O I E M T D
G H T J S I N O P M R F G M H
W Y D E L R K V M Z Q Y B S G
W F C S D W N I Z E K S I I P
A E G M X E U W N X S Y Q V N
R V F Y V A L W H I Y O H L I
J A B J W C G P S X A Z W X B
```

100% Curriculum Vocabulary—Grades 6-12

3 Definitions — Biology

1. **alveoli** — air sacs in the lungs

2. **antibiotics** — medicines used to kill bacteria that cause disease

3. **antibody** — a substance, produced in the blood or tissues, that kills or weakens bacteria

4. **antigen** — a substance that causes the body to produce antibodies to fight disease

5. **artery** — a tube that carries blood away from the heart to all parts of the body

6. **bacteria** — single cells that cause disease or help to protect the body from disease

7. **capillary** — the smallest blood vessel that joins the end of an artery to the beginning of a vein

8. **clot** — lump or mass formed by thickened blood

9. **immunity** — the body's ability to produce antibodies to protect itself from disease

10. **marrow** — soft material inside bones that produces red blood cells

3 Fill-in-the-Blank — Biology

Fill in the blanks with the words from the box.

| marrow | alveoli | capillary | immunity | bacteria |
| artery | clot | antigen | antibiotics | antibody |

1. _____ are cells that cause disease or help to protect the body from disease.

2. A substance that causes the body to produce antibodies is an _____.

3. An _____ is a blood vessel that carries blood away from the heart.

4. _____ are small air sacs in the lungs.

5. Medicines that kill bacteria that cause disease are _____.

6. An _____ is produced in the blood or tissues and kills bacteria.

7. Red blood cells produced by _____ are found inside your bones.

8. A _____ is the smallest blood vessel that joins the end of an artery to the beginning of a vein.

9. A _____ is a lump or mass formed by thickened blood.

10. _____ is the body's way to produce antibodies to protect itself from disease.

3 Word Association — Biology

Write the word from the box next to the word or phrase that shares a similar meaning.

| marrow | alveoli | capillary | immunity | bacteria |
| artery | clot | antigen | antibiotics | antibody |

1. medicines _____

2. lump or thickened blood _____

3. kills bacteria _____

4. produces antibodies _____

5. air sacs _____

6. smallest blood vessel _____

7. causes disease _____

8. carries blood away from heart _____

9. body's way to protect itself _____

10. soft material inside bones _____

3 Writing Sentences — Biology

Write a sentence using each word.

1. alveoli

2. antibiotics

3. antibody

4. antigen

5. artery

6. bacteria

7. capillary

8. clot

9. immunity

10. marrow

Crossword Puzzle — Biology

Complete the puzzle with words that match the clues.

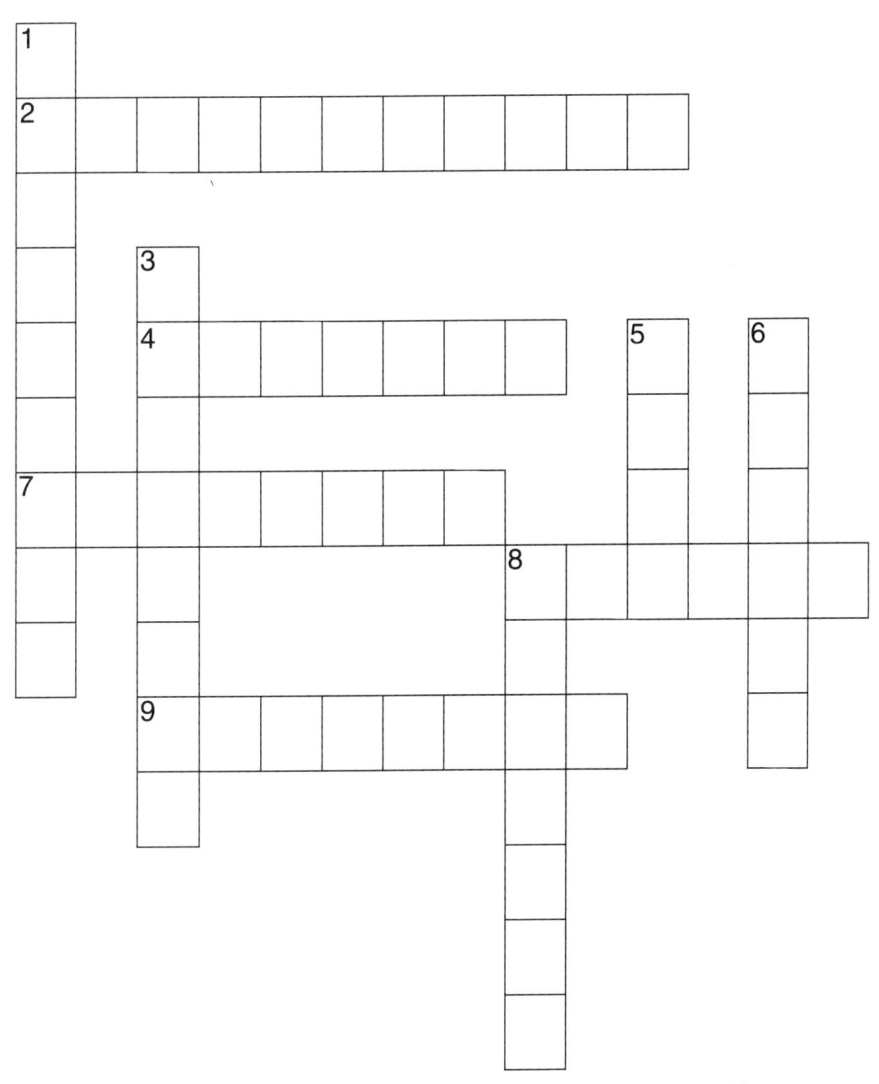

Across

2. medicines used to kill bacteria that cause disease
4. air sacs in the lungs
7. a substance produced in the blood or tissues that kills or weakens bacteria
8. a tube that carries blood away from the heart to all parts of the body
9. the body's ability to produce antibodies to protect itself from disease

Down

1. the smallest blood vessel that joins the end of an artery to the beginning of a vein
3. single cells that cause disease or help to protect the body from disease
5. thickened blood that forms a lump or mass
6. soft material inside bones that produces red blood cells
8. a substance that causes the body to produce antibodies to fight disease

Word Search — Biology

All the words or phrases listed in the box appear in the puzzle — horizontally, vertically, diagonally, or backward. Find and circle them.

marrow	alveoli	capillary	immunity	bacteria
artery	clot	antigen	antibiotics	antibody

```
A T K Y J S V C M C Y C I Q G
K N Y Q C V G H L A V C G J Y
A Y T I N U M M I P R K C T Y
M I J I G M Z V I I E R L M X
Q T R H B X J O B L L T O U R
W N V E Z I C U Q L W U T W I
F E N G T R O A I A Q L P L H
W G Q M N C N T W R T D O V I
K I H L S T A E I Y R E J W E
O T E G I U L B S C V I Q Y K
Y N X B B O H V Q L S Y Y N A
X A O F V A E R A A R T E R Y
U D E O B C D M I S J T X C D
Y W J J S K F T V M A N I V P
W E Y U F Q G C T S A Y F Y B
```

100% Curriculum Vocabulary—Grades 6-12

Definitions — Biology

1. **carnivore** — an animal that only eats meat

2. **consumer** — a living thing that does not produce its own food

3. **decomposer** — a living thing that eats dead animals, plants, and waste

4. **food chain** — a series of steps that lets food and energy move through the environment

5. **herbivore** — an animal that only eats plants

6. **invertebrate** — an animal without a backbone, such as a worm

7. **organism** — a living thing that can carry on the processes of life

8. **parasite** — an organism that lives on or in another organism and hurts it by taking away food

9. **producer** — an organism, such as a green plant, that is able to make its own food

10. **venom** — poison found in an animal, such as a snake or spider, that is passed to a victim by biting or stinging

4 Fill-in-the-Blank — Biology

Fill in the blanks with the words or phrases from the box.

venom	carnivore	invertebrate	herbivore	food chain
organism	producer	parasite	consumer	decomposer

1. Another word for *poison* is _____.

2. A _____ is a living thing that does not produce its own food.

3. A cow is an example of a _____ because it only eats plants.

4. A _____ is a living thing that eats dead animals, plants, and waste.

5. An example of an _____ is a worm because it has no backbone.

6. The _____ is a series of steps that lets food and energy move through the environment.

7. A plant is a _____ because it is able to make its own food.

8. An organism that lives on or in another organism and hurts it by taking away food is a _____.

9. A _____ is an animal that only eats meat.

10. A living thing that carries on life processes is an _____.

4 Word Association — Biology

Write the word or phrase from the box next to the word or phrase that shares a similar meaning.

venom	carnivore	invertebrate	herbivore	food chain
organism	producer	parasite	consumer	decomposer

1. meat eater _____

2. eats dead animals _____

3. living thing _____

4. makes its own food _____

5. plant eater _____

6. poison _____

7. without a backbone _____

8. food and energy moving through environment _____

9. doesn't produce own food _____

10. hurts another organism by taking away food _____

4 Writing Sentences — Biology

Write a sentence using each word or phrase.

1. carnivore

2. consumer

3. decomposer

4. food chain

5. herbivore

6. invertebrate

7. organism

8. parasite

9. producer

10. venom

Crossword Puzzle — Biology

Complete the puzzle with words that match the clues.

Across

2. a series of steps that lets food and energy move through the environment
6. a living thing that eats dead animals, plants, and waste
7. poison found in an animal that is passed to a victim by biting or stinging
9. an animal that only eats plants
10. an organism that lives on or in another organism and hurts it by taking away food

Down

1. an animal without a backbone, such as a worm
3. an animal that only eats meat
4. an organism, such as a green plant, that is able to make its own food
5. a living thing that does not produce its own food
8. a living thing that can carry on the processes of life

4 Word Search — Biology

All the words or phrases listed in the box appear in the puzzle — horizontally, vertically, diagonally, or backward. Find and circle them.

venom	carnivore	invertebrate	herbivore	food chain
organism	producer	parasite	consumer	decomposer

```
N B R Z G Z C Z Q F I E X E R
Z R E E R C E A O M T P T X E
I J D G M U U O R A S I B U C
V T N U W U D T R N S M I B U
T B E D C C S B O A I K L I D
P H E M H N E N R V W V K Y O
E G O A W T O A O D Z H O M R
W K I Y R X P O T C S E K R P
E N D E C O M P O S E R X N E
H O V M S I N A G R O B P G O
L N V E N O M A W C W I I U E
I F J J N F O M H V F V I T X
D M X U O G S H I F F O Z F C
A K Q V D D K X A L A R W T N
B G Q D Q O X C N Q T E L C I
```

100% Curriculum Vocabulary—Grades 6-12

5 Definitions — Biology

1. **anterior** — relates to the front section of an object or an animal

2. **cartilage** — tough, stretchy substance connected to bones that forms parts of the skeleton, such as the ear

3. **central nervous system** — the part of the nervous system made up of the brain and the spinal cord

4. **disease** — a sickness or illness

5. **element** — a substance that is made of only one type of atom

6. **embryo** — a person before birth or an animal before hatching

7. **joint** — the point where a bone connects with another bone

8. **molecule** — two or more atoms joined together

9. **posterior** — relates to the rear section of an object or an animal

10. **virus** — a substance that infects the cells in our bodies and causes illnesses, such as chicken pox and the flu

5 Fill-in-the-Blank — Biology

Fill in the blanks with the words or phrases from the box.

| disease | anterior | central nervous system | posterior | cartilage |
| virus | embryo | molecule | element | joint |

1. A _____ is the point where a bone connects with another bone.

2. The _____ part of an animal relates to the front section of the animal.

3. The ear is made of a tough, stretchy substance called _____.

4. A _____ is two or more atoms joined together.

5. The _____ is made up of the brain and the spinal cord.

6. A _____ infects the cells in our bodies and causes illnesses, such as chicken pox and the flu.

7. An _____ is a substance made up of one type of atom.

8. A person before birth or an animal before hatching is an _____.

9. Another word for *sickness* is _____.

10. The _____ part of an animal relates to the rear section of the animal.

5 Word Association — Biology

Write the word or phrase from the box next to the word or phrase that shares a similar meaning.

disease	anterior	central nervous system	posterior	cartilage
virus	embryo	molecule	element	joint

1. brain and spinal cord　　_____

2. stretchy substance　　_____

3. sickness　　_____

4. single atom　　_____

5. unborn child or animal　　_____

6. point where bones connect　　_____

7. front part　　_____

8. atoms joined together　　_____

9. rear part　　_____

10. causes illness　　_____

5 Writing Sentences — Biology

Write a sentence using each word or phrase.

1. anterior

2. cartilage

3. central nervous system

4. disease

5. element

6. embryo

7. joint

8. molecule

9. posterior

10. virus

Crossword Puzzle 5

Biology

Complete the puzzle with words that match the clues.

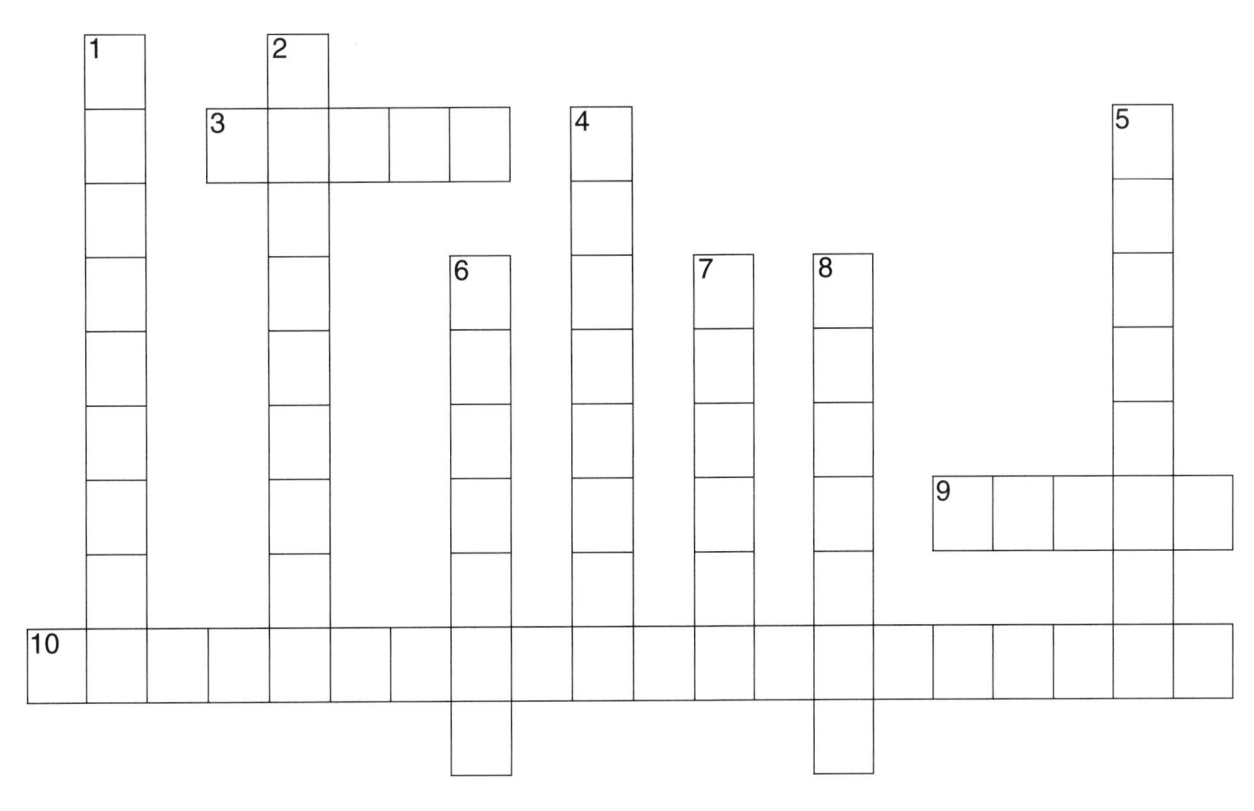

Across

3. the point where a bone connects with another bone
9. a substance that infects the cells in our bodies and causes illnesses, such as chicken pox and the flu
10. the part of the nervous system made up of the brain and the spinal cord

Down

1. tough, stretchy substance connected to bones that forms parts of the skeleton
2. relates to the rear section of an object or an animal
4. relates to the front section of an object or an animal
5. two or more atoms joined together
6. a substance that is made of only one type of atom
7. a person before birth or an animal before hatching
8. a sickness or illness

5 Word Search — Biology

All the words or phrases listed in the box appear in the puzzle — horizontally, vertically, diagonally, or backward. Find and circle them.

disease	anterior	central nervous system	posterior	cartilage
virus	embryo	molecule	element	joint

```
E E J J W R J B C R C I I E N A E P U D
Y M B H I T E W E P O L O L G B I I T F
E D B N R S Y P N Y E I F U Q R Y D H Q
H R F R A M I G T U E I R C Y E P R K P
D U Y E Y J Z B R H J F U E U Q X B H L
W F S V B O D C A I O K G L T Y S P P E
G I K E V N J F L X I W S O J N J F Y Z
D V Z F S F G P N Y N E U M Z V A W A Z
D C A B E L E M E N T U S R U W Z P L T
K J K V M J G Z R G V V S T H R O N M W
Y A L A O L N U V O U V I U N S N Q U E
Z I W U V Z P U O P P I B L T F G H E Y
I M P D V W V V U U B W G E K X P L T I
I N D I P G M Y S A T G R P N J U O I N
E I R Q X H M X S B C I M U W N X S U R
S U U M H A S L Y L O E G A L I T R A C
S W J A M O C V S R I T U B S J V M C J
K G P X E G A R T A P N P D N D V K E Y
P Z A Z X K Y E A U C W I C R W O U J
O F P X N C D B M U F K W Z Z D R N P X
```

1 Definitions — Consumer

1. **adjust** — to change something to make it more satisfactory

2. **balance** — the amount of money in a checking or savings account

3. **biweekly** — happens every two weeks

4. **checking account** — a bank account with checks that are used to pay bills

5. **expenditure** — an amount of money spent for bills, food, etc.

6. **gross pay** — the total amount of money an employee earns

7. **interest** — the amount of money paid to borrow someone else's money, usually a percentage of the borrowed amount

8. **net pay** — the amount of money an employee earns after money has been withheld for taxes and deductions

9. **salary** — the fixed amount of money a worker earns for doing a job

10. **withhold** — to hold back taxes and other deductions from a paycheck

1 Fill-in-the-Blank — Consumer

Fill in the blanks with the words or phrases from the box.

| adjust | balance | checking account | biweekly | expenditure |
| net pay | interest | gross pay | salary | withhold |

1. A _____ is a bank account with checks that are used to pay bills.

2. To deduct taxes from a paycheck is to _____.

3. An _____ is an amount of money spent for bills, food, etc.

4. _____ means every two weeks.

5. The total amount of money paid to an employee is her _____.

6. The amount of money in a bank account is the _____.

7. When you _____ something, you change it to make it more satisfactory.

8. The amount of money an employee earns after taxes and deductions are taken out is his _____.

9. A _____ is the amount of money a worker earns for doing a job.

10. Sometimes you pay _____ when you borrow money.

1 Word Association — Consumer

Write the word or phrase from the box next to the word or phrase that shares a similar meaning.

| adjust | balance | checking account | biweekly | expenditure |
| net pay | interest | gross pay | salary | withhold |

1. amount of money in a bank account _____

2. every two weeks _____

3. to deduct _____

4. fixed amount earned _____

5. a bill _____

6. total amount earned _____

7. money paid to borrow money _____

8. amount earned after taxes are taken out _____

9. bank account with checks _____

10. change _____

1 Writing Sentences — Consumer

Write a sentence using each word or phrase.

1. adjust

2. balance

3. biweekly

4. checking account

5. expenditure

6. gross pay

7. interest

8. net pay

9. salary

10. withhold

Crossword Puzzle — Consumer

Complete the puzzle with words that match the clues.

Across

4. the fixed amount of money a worker earns for doing a job
6. happens every two weeks
8. the amount of money an employee earns after money has been withheld for taxes and deductions
9. a bank account with checks that are used to pay bills

Down

1. the total amount of money an employee earns
2. an amount of money spent for bills, food, etc.
3. the amount of money paid to borrow someone else's money, usually a percentage of the borrowed amount
5. to hold back taxes and other deductions from a paycheck
7. the amount of money in a checking or savings account
10. to change something to make it more satisfactory

1 Word Search — Consumer

All the words or phrases listed in the box appear in the puzzle — horizontally, vertically, diagonally, or backward. Find and circle them.

adjust	balance	checking account	biweekly	expenditure
net pay	interest	gross pay	salary	withhold

```
E X P E N D I T U R E V G E T
I O U O C T R X V Y F R W N B
X N R S S N P Y R Y O D U T I
F T T W J V A A G S O O G S W
S J H E X B L L S N C V O U E
D J H I R A X P A C H B R J E
D C M F S E A G A B M F N D K
N E T P A Y S G C D C Q R A L
Z D E K V R N T O N E C I O Y
G J Y L M I D L O H H T I W H
T N V O K D A W L Z M R J J B
G D O C D E B E G E N S G M R
D P E A P W E B K B Y X W A I
C H D V K T T J T B Z N B E E
C R O E T G D Q A W I Y M L V
```

100% Curriculum Vocabulary—Grades 6-12   Copyright © 2002 LinguiSystems, Inc.

② Definitions — Consumer

1. **address** — the place where someone lives or works, including the number, street, city, state, and ZIP code

2. **application** — a form a person fills out when trying to get a job

3. **company** — a group of people working together to do business

4. **employee** — a person who works for a company; also called a *worker*

5. **interview** — a meeting where a person is asked questions to find out if he/she is qualified for a job

6. **position** — the name of the job that an employee does

7. **promotion** — a raise in position that may include an increase in salary

8. **résumé** — a short written list of a person's previous jobs, qualifications, and education that is used when applying for a job

9. **schedule** — a written plan that shows the time and order of each job and who does each job

10. **time card** — a card used with a time clock to stamp an employee's starting and ending times

② Fill-in-the-Blank — Consumer

Fill in the blanks with the words or phrases from the box.

> address　　schedule　　company　　promotion　　interview
> résumé　　application　　time card　　employee　　position

1. A _____ is a raise in a worker's position that may result in an increase in pay.

2. A _____ is a group of people working together to do business.

3. A plan that shows what days people work is a _____.

4. My _____ is 2808 East Pleasant Street, Davenport, IA, 52803.

5. An _____ is a meeting where a person is asked questions to find out if he/she is qualified for a job.

6. A card used with a time clock is a _____.

7. A _____ is a written list of a person's previous jobs.

8. A person who is working is an _____.

9. The name of the job an employee does is his _____.

10. An _____ is a form a person fills out when he/she is trying to get a job.

2 Word Association — Consumer

Write the word or phrase from the box next to the word or phrase that shares a similar meaning.

> address　　schedule　　company　　promotion　　interview
> résumé　　application　　time card　　employee　　position

1. name of job　　_____

2. raise in position　　_____

3. 3100 4th Avenue　　_____

4. worker　　_____

5. people working together　　_____

6. form for a job　　_____

7. written list of previous jobs　　_____

8. written plan to show time and order　　_____

9. card used to mark starting and ending times　　_____

10. meeting　　_____

2 Writing Sentences — Consumer

Write a sentence using each word or phrase.

1. address

2. application

3. company

4. employee

5. interview

6. position

7. promotion

8. résumé

9. schedule

10. time card

Crossword Puzzle — Consumer

Complete the puzzle with words that match the clues.

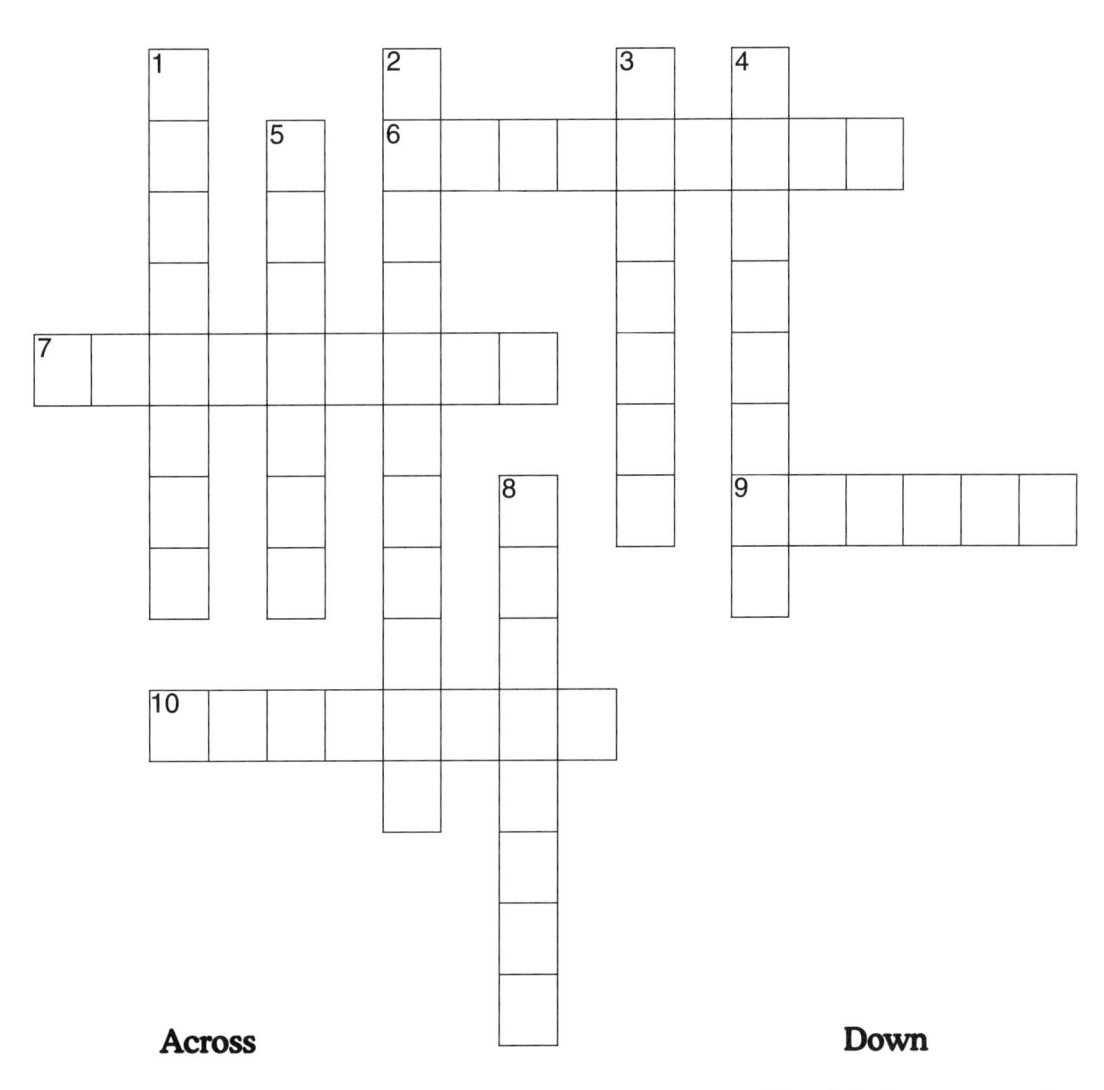

Across

6. a raise in position that may include an increase in salary
7. a meeting where a person is asked questions to find out if he is qualified for a job
9. a short written list of a person's previous jobs, qualifications, and education that is used when applying for a job
10. a person who works for a company, also called a *worker*

Down

1. the name of the job that an employee does
2. a form a person fills out when trying to get a job
3. a group of people working together to do business
4. a card used with a time clock to stamp an employee's starting and ending times
5. the place where someone lives or works, including the number, street, city, state, and ZIP code
8. a written plan that shows the time and order of each job and who does each job

② Word Search — Consumer

All the words or phrases listed in the box appear in the puzzle — horizontally, vertically, diagonally, or backward. Find and circle them.

address	schedule	company	promotion	interview
résumé	application	time card	employee	position

```
I A D J I D M F P G D E Z G I
M Z P P I N C R Q R F L A N N
Z P X P D M O G A V Y U V H T
P C Y K L M N C F R G D P R E
I K B O O I E O F L G E L K R
R K T T I M C I I B Y H P I V
A R I Y I Z C A K T O C L M I
F O F T B I C O T A I S S K E
N A D D R E S S M I M S J D W
S X H A N J J S T P O B O N R
Z D M R D X T H H Q A N Z P E
O E E Y O L P M E F I N B D S
Y P V I H L E Y U Z P A Y U U
M Z L Z U R V T V P W M O Y M
O G V V F Q W I E Y W S A O E
```

100% Curriculum Vocabulary—Grades 6-12   Copyright © 2002 LinguiSystems, Inc.

3 Definitions — Consumer

1. **advertisement** something on TV or radio or in a magazine or newspaper that tells people why they should buy a product or service

2. **credit card** a plastic card that allows people to buy goods and services by paying for them at a later date

3. **discount** an amount that is less than the regular or full price

4. **identification** something used to prove who a person is, usually with a picture of the person on it (driver's license, school I.D.)

5. **lease** a written agreement to rent something

6. **mean** the average of a group of numbers

7. **mortgage** the amount of money paid each month to pay off a property loan

8. **odds** the ratio of wins to losses for an event

9. **rent** the amount of money paid each month to use a property

10. **sale price** the discounted price of an item

3 Fill-in-the-Blank — Consumer

Fill in the blanks with the words or phrases from the box.

| lease | discount | identification | credit card | odds |
| mortgage | rent | advertisement | mean | sale price |

1. When writing a check, a person has to show his/her _____ to prove who they are.

2. The discounted price of an item is a _____.

3. Money paid every month to use a property is _____.

4. A _____ is an amount that is less than the regular or full price.

5. A plastic card used to buy things is a _____.

6. A _____ is a written agreement to rent something.

7. The ratio of success to failure for an event is the _____.

8. The money paid every month to own a property is the _____.

9. An _____ tells people why they should buy a product or service.

10. The average of a group of numbers is the _____.

3 Word Association — Consumer

Write the word or phrase from the box next to the word or phrase that shares a similar meaning.

lease	discount	identification	credit card	odds
mortgage	rent	advertisement	mean	sale price

1. average _____

2. written agreement to rent _____

3. money paid to use something _____

4. ratio _____

5. proof with a picture _____

6. money paid for a property loan _____

7. amount less than full price _____

8. buy now and pay later _____

9. tells you to buy a product _____

10. discounted price of an item _____

3 Writing Sentences — Consumer

Write a sentence using each word or phrase.

1. advertisement

2. credit card

3. discount

4. identification

5. lease

6. mean

7. mortgage

8. odds

9. rent

10. sale price

③ Crossword Puzzle — Consumer

Complete the puzzle with words that match the clues.

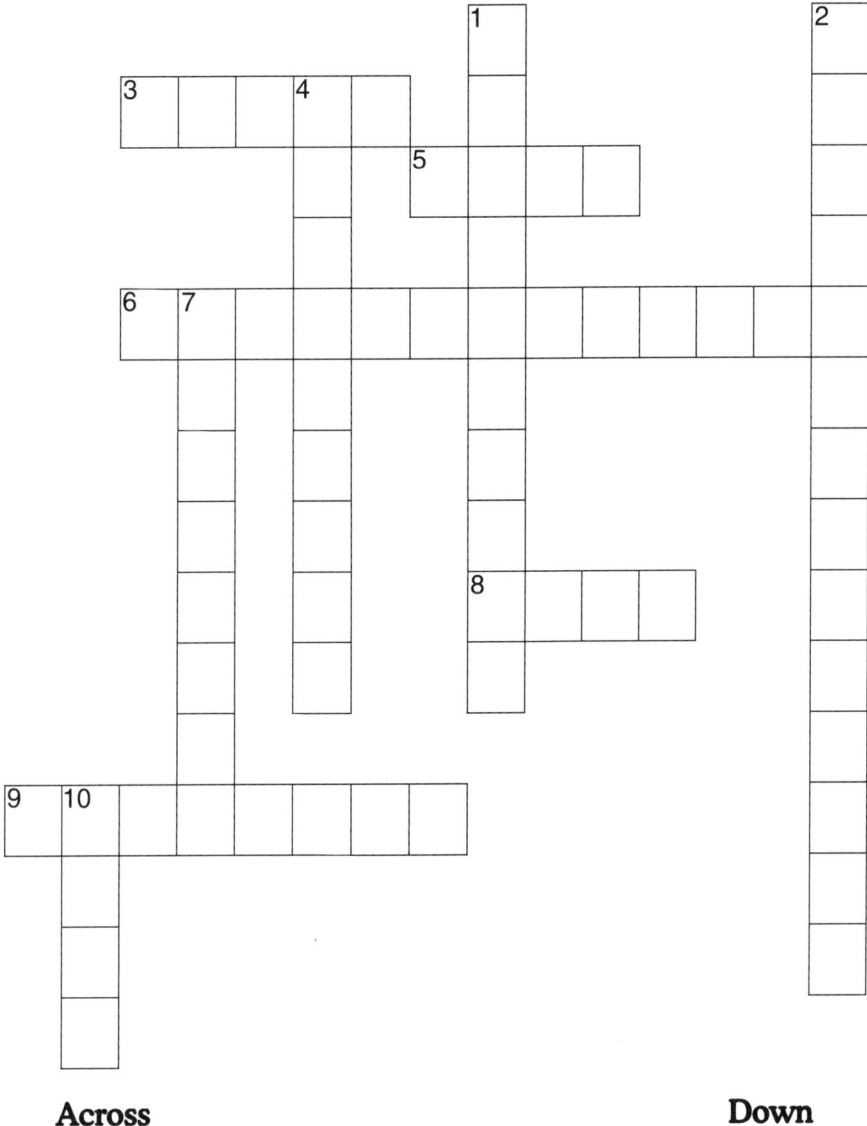

Across

3. a written agreement to rent something
5. the average of a group of numbers
6. something on TV or radio that tells people why they should buy a product or service
8. the amount of money paid each month to use a property
9. the amount of money paid each month to pay off a property loan

Down

1. a plastic card that allows people to buy goods and services by paying for them at a later date
2. something used to prove who a person is, usually with a picture of the person
4. the discounted price of an item
7. an amount that is less than the regular or full price
10. the ratio of wins to losses for an event

3 Word Search — Consumer

All the words or phrases listed in the box appear in the puzzle — horizontally, vertically, diagonally, or backward. Find and circle them.

lease	discount	identification	credit card	odds
mortgage	rent	advertisement	mean	sale price

```
A D V E R T I S E M E N T D S
K Z O L Q N N J P D N D I D C
I Z Z B Z O A R G R I S D M K
K C O K C I E O Y D C O E L B
S F R P F T M O Y O R I M L S
Z M Y E X A N Z U N F Q I M S
I J M S D C O N N P L Y T E E
P K M A U I T E G A G T R O M
E N V L V F T R E N T H Y I C
I M E E K I B C K B Y Z H Y I
K X V P O T E C A R E S F A I
F H E R Z N B S N R G L T M M
Q T V I R E R D A L D A M L R
D T V C B D J E O E B D Y M D
W H Z E B I Y R F P L Z U I F
```

100% Curriculum Vocabulary—Grades 6–12

4 Definitions — Consumer

1. **car pool** a group of workers who travel together by car to and from work

2. **detour** a route that is different from the regular way

3. **lane** a part of a road for a single line of traffic

4. **merge** to gradually move your vehicle into an existing lane of traffic

5. **pedestrian** a person who is walking

6. **prohibited** not allowed (e.g., Driving on sidewalks is prohibited.)

7. **residential** an area where there are homes instead of businesses

8. **restriction** a limit or rule

9. **shoulder** the area on either side of a road that is outside the traveled area; the edge of a road

10. **visibility** the ability to have a clear view of the road

4 Fill-in-the-Blank — Consumer

Fill in the blanks with the words or phrases from the box.

| car pool | shoulder | residential | prohibited | lane |
| detour | visibility | pedestrian | restriction | merge |

1. The edge of the road is the _____.

2. A limit or a rule is a _____.

3. If you choose to pass another car, you should use the left _____.

4. A driver will _____ when he moves his vehicle into an existing lane of traffic.

5. A _____ is a person who is walking.

6. When it is foggy outside, the _____ of the road becomes worse.

7. A _____ area has homes in it instead of businesses.

8. A _____ is a route that is different than the regular way.

9. Driving on the sidewalk is _____.

10. A _____ is a group of workers who travel together by car to and from work.

4 Word Association — Consumer

Write the word or phrase from the box next to the word or phrase that shares a similar meaning.

| car pool | shoulder | residential | prohibited | lane |
| detour | visibility | pedestrian | restriction | merge |

1. area with homes _____

2. gradually move into one lane _____

3. person walking _____

4. not allowed _____

5. edge of road _____

6. travel together by car _____

7. different route _____

8. rule _____

9. clear view _____

10. part of the road for traffic _____

4 Writing Sentences — Consumer

Write a sentence using each word or phrase.

1. car pool _____

2. detour _____

3. lane _____

4. merge _____

5. pedestrian _____

6. prohibited _____

7. residential _____

8. restriction _____

9. shoulder _____

10. visibility _____

4 Crossword Puzzle — Consumer

Complete the puzzle with words that match the clues.

Across

1. a person who is walking
4. the ability to have a clear view of the road
7. a group of workers who travel together by car to and from work
9. a route that is different from the regular way
10. an area where there are homes instead of businesses

Down

2. a limit or rule
3. not allowed
5. to gradually move your vehicle into an existing lane of traffic
6. the edge of a road
8. a part of a road for a single line of traffic

4 Word Search — Consumer

All the words or phrases listed in the box appear in the puzzle — horizontally, vertically, diagonally, or backward. Find and circle them.

| car pool | shoulder | residential | prohibited | lane |
| detour | visibility | pedestrian | restriction | merge |

```
N D V D L K S G R I R N H R Y
B T E A E V S E K E P T F E T
G M F T T T D W S O V M A S I
G E M N O L I T H O L N Z I L
Q R U S U U R B R X G R B D I
G G C O D I R F I M K G X E B
L E H S C D G V P H K P Q N I
Y S G T L C A R P O O L Q T S
T X I A Q Y T Q S J X R Y I I
L O N A I R T S E D E P P A V
N E E S L T Z E R Q H X P L L
B C P W Q V G U W R P I L M X
O Q N D A D U E R F P Y G C H
A P O O J J Z N J A F K B A G
L R G S W I U T E S G X S O D
```

Definitions — Earth Science

1. **atmosphere** — the air that surrounds Earth

2. **barometer** — a tool used to determine changes in the weather by measuring the amount of pressure in the air

3. **Celsius** — a measurement of temperature in which 0 degrees is the freezing point of water and 100 degrees is the boiling point of water

4. **climate** — the usual kind of weather a place has

5. **evaporation** — the process of a liquid turning into a gas

6. **Fahrenheit** — a measurement of the temperature in which 32 degrees is the freezing point of water and 212 degrees is the boiling point of water

7. **hurricane** — a destructive storm with strong winds and heavy rains that forms over a warm ocean

8. **precipitation** — when liquid or solid water returns to Earth in the form of rain, hail, sleet, or snow

9. **saturated** — completely full of moisture; 100% humidity in the air

10. **tornado** — a violent, destructive windstorm that creates a dark, funnel-shaped cloud that forms over land

1 Fill-in-the-Blank — Earth Science

Fill in the blanks with the words from the box.

| climate | saturated | atmosphere | evaporation | barometer |
| tornado | hurricane | precipitation | Fahrenheit | Celsius |

1. The boiling point of water is 212 degrees _____.

2. A _____ is a violent windstorm that forms over land.

3. The freezing point of water is 0 degrees _____.

4. The _____ is the air around the earth.

5. A destructive storm with strong winds and heavy rains that forms over an ocean is a _____.

6. _____ happens when a liquid turns into a gas.

7. When there is 100% humidity in the air, the air is said to be _____.

8. A tool used to measure the amount of pressure in the air is a _____.

9. Rain, hail, sleet, or snow returns to Earth as _____.

10. The usual kind of weather a place has is its _____.

100% Curriculum Vocabulary—Grades 6-12   86   Copyright © 2002 LinguiSystems, Inc.

1 Word Association — Earth Science

Write the word from the box next to the word or phrase that shares a similar meaning.

| climate | saturated | atmosphere | evaporation | barometer |
| tornado | hurricane | precipitation | Fahrenheit | Celsius |

1. liquid into gas _____

2. freezing point at 0 degrees _____

3. usual weather _____

4. windstorm over land _____

5. full of moisture _____

6. ocean storm _____

7. Earth's air _____

8. freezing point at 32 degrees _____

9. measures air pressure _____

10. rain, sleet, or snow _____

1 Writing Sentences — Earth Science

Write a sentence using each word.

1. atmosphere

2. barometer

3. Celsius

4. climate

5. evaporation

6. Fahrenheit

7. hurricane

8. precipitation

9. saturated

10. tornado

Crossword Puzzle — Earth Science

Complete the puzzle with words that match the clues.

Across

1. the process of a liquid turning into a gas
6. a measurement of the temperature in which 32 degrees is the freezing point of water and 212 degrees is the boiling point of water
9. a measurement of temperature in which 0 degrees is the freezing point of water and 100 degrees is the boiling point of water
10. the usual kind of weather a place has

Down

2. when liquid or solid water returns to Earth in the form of rain, hail, sleet, or snow
3. the air that surrounds Earth
4. a tool used to determine changes in the weather by measuring the amount of pressure in the air
5. completely full of moisture; 100% humidity
7. a destructive storm with strong winds and heavy rains that forms over a warm ocean
8. a violent, destructive windstorm that creates a dark, funnel-shaped cloud that forms over land

100% Curriculum Vocabulary—Grades 6-12

1. Word Search — Earth Science

All the words or phrases listed in the box appear in the puzzle — horizontally, vertically, diagonally, or backward. Find and circle them.

climate	saturated	atmosphere	evaporation	barometer
tornado	hurricane	precipitation	Fahrenheit	Celsius

```
E V C Y E Z P E A A I F T O
N H Y L S V X X T E D T A O F
A E S J I N A M X O A K H R Y
C T X P B M O P S J M C R N S
I F T C N S A P O H Y F E A W
R A B N P O P T P R I Y N D A
R W F H R F Q Z E M A D H O O
U R E T E M O R A B E T E G R
H R P R E C I P I T A T I O N
E C E L S I U S A D H C T O D
D O V O D W G R R V S Z T H N
B N F U Z R U Z R S M A U C J
O U N G T T U U T P M H T E E
J I D H A Z S Q E O R D X C C
U N U S U P G P X T W S Y U P
```

100% Curriculum Vocabulary—Grades 6-12   Copyright © 2002 LinguiSystems, Inc.

Definitions — Earth Science

1. **asteroid** — a small rock found in outer space, mostly between Mars and Jupiter

2. **astronomer** — a scientist who studies outer space

3. **black hole** — an object in outer space with a pull of gravity so strong that nothing can escape it, not even light; acts like a vacuum cleaner

4. **constellation** — a group of stars that forms a shape or pattern, such as the Big Dipper

5. **galaxy** — a group of stars that is held together by gravity and forms one system

6. **meteor** — a piece of rock or metal from space that enters Earth's atmosphere with great speed; also called a *shooting star* because it looks like a streak of light

7. **nebula** — a huge cloud of gas and dust found in space

8. **orbit** — the path of an object in outer space as it moves in a circle around another object (e.g., Earth's orbit around the Sun)

9. **planet** — a large body that moves in an orbit around the Sun, such as Neptune, Earth, and Saturn

10. **supernova** — a star that breaks apart in an explosion

② Fill-in-the-Blank — Earth Science

Fill in the blanks with the words or phrases from the box.

asteroid	black hole	supernova	constellation	nebula
galaxy	planet	astronomer	meteor	orbit

1. A _____ is a huge cloud of gas and dust found in space.

2. An exploding star is a _____.

3. An _____ is a small rock in outer space.

4. The _____ of an object is the path it takes as it moves in a circle around another object.

5. The pull of gravity in a _____ is so strong that nothing can escape it.

6. Another name for a shooting star is a _____.

7. A group of stars that is held together by gravity and forms one system is a _____.

8. Neptune is a _____.

9. A group of stars that forms a shape, such as the Big Dipper, is a _____.

10. An _____ is a scientist who studies outer space.

② Word Association — Earth Science

Write the word or phrase from the box next to the word or phrase that shares a similar meaning.

| asteroid | black hole | supernova | constellation | nebula |
| galaxy | planet | astronomer | meteor | orbit |

1. shooting star _____

2. pattern of stars _____

3. group of stars _____

4. scientist who studies outer space _____

5. object with strong gravity _____

6. path _____

7. exploding star _____

8. cloud of gas _____

9. rock in outer space _____

10. Saturn _____

② Writing Sentences — Earth Science

Write a sentence using each word or phrase.

1. asteroid

2. astronomer

3. black hole

4. constellation

5. galaxy

6. meteor

7. nebula

8. orbit

9. planet

10. supernova

Crossword Puzzle — Earth Science

Complete the puzzle with words that match the clues.

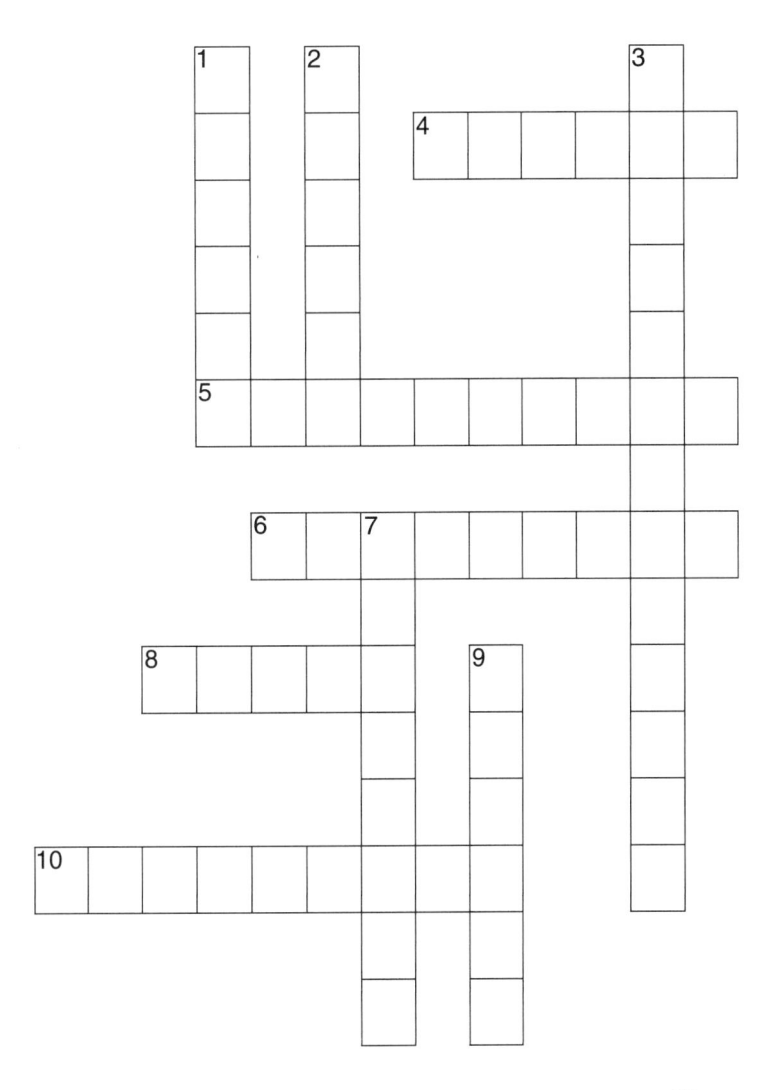

Across

4. a piece of rock or metal from space that enters Earth's atmosphere with great speed; also called a *shooting star*
5. a scientist who studies outer space
6. an object in outer space with a pull of gravity so strong that nothing can escape it, not even light
8. the path of an object in outer space as it moves in a circle around another object
10. a star that breaks apart in an explosion

Down

1. a huge cloud of gas and dust found in space
2. a large body that moves in an orbit around the Sun, such as Neptune, Earth, and Saturn
3. a group of stars that forms a shape or pattern, such as the Big Dipper
7. a rock found in outer space
9. a group of stars that is held together by gravity and forms one system

② Word Search — Earth Science

All the words or phrases listed in the box appear in the puzzle — horizontally, vertically, diagonally, or backward. Find and circle them.

asteroid	black hole	supernova	constellation	nebula
galaxy	planet	astronomer	meteor	orbit

```
Q A B O Q G T P S N A I X R A
B P R W T H S Y U O L U U N A
G L K O Z U O V P I U A F E R
J M A S E I Y I E T B H L M M
D H Y C G T P Z R A E Y N F Z
S C B B K U E A N L N Y L I T
A V O C E H S M O L O R B I T
Y S R L B T O V V E G K U C Y
V A F R E U U L A T V C W Z P
H I S R Z K F L E S W V A Z T
W J O Y X A L A G N Z V K E R
N I Z P E A U S Z O R W N O E
D T V Q L Y R W O C H A U F R
A S T R O N O M E R L X D Y N
I K V U V A Y C H P Q B W B R
```

3 Definitions — Earth Science

1. **anther** — the part of the flower's stem that holds the pollen

2. **deciduous** — a kind of tree with leaves that fall off each autumn and grow back each spring

3. **fruit** — the part of a flower or tree that holds seeds and is usually good to eat, such as an apple or a peach

4. **photosynthesis** — the process by which plants make their own food by using energy from the sun

5. **pistil** — the central part of a flower where the seeds are made

6. **pollen** — a yellowish powder found in a flower that must be carried from a stamen to a pistil in order for seeds to form

7. **roots** — the underground part of a plant that grows down into the soil and holds the plant in place while the plant absorbs water and nutrients

8. **seed** — the part of a plant that can grow into a new plant

9. **stamen** — the stem part of a flower that makes pollen and is surrounded by petals

10. **stem** — the main part of a plant above the ground that supports the leaves and flowers; carries water to the leaves and flowers

100% Curriculum Vocabulary—Grades 6-12   Copyright © 2002 LinguiSystems, Inc.

3. Fill-in-the-Blank — Earth Science

Fill in the blanks with the words from the box.

anther	seed	deciduous	pollen	roots
stamen	stem	photosynthesis	pistil	fruit

1. The yellowish powder that must be carried from a stamen to a pistil in order for seeds to form is _____.

2. A _____ tree has leaves that fall off each autumn and grow back.

3. The stem part of the flower that makes pollen is the _____.

4. A _____ is the part of a plant that can grow into a new plant.

5. The central part of a flower where the seeds are made is the _____.

6. The _____ of a plant grow down into the soil and hold the plant in place while the plant absorbs water and nutrients.

7. The _____ is the part of the flower's stem that holds the pollen.

8. The process by which plants make their own food by using energy from the sun is called _____.

9. The main part of a plant that supports the leaves and flowers is the _____.

10. _____ holds the seeds of a flower and is usually good to eat.

3 Word Association — Earth Science

Write the word from the box next to the word or phrase that shares a similar meaning.

anther	seed	deciduous	pollen	roots
stamen	stem	photosynthesis	pistil	fruit

1. holds pollen _____

2. kind of tree _____

3. makes seeds _____

4. underground part of plant _____

5. makes pollen _____

6. yellowish powder _____

7. energy from the sun _____

8. main part of a plant _____

9. part that holds seeds _____

10. can grow into a new plant _____

3 Writing Sentences — Earth Science

Write a sentence using each word.

1. anther

2. deciduous

3. fruit

4. photosynthesis

5. pistil

6. pollen

7. roots

8. seed

9. stamen

10. stem

3 Crossword Puzzle — Earth Science

Complete the puzzle with words that match the clues.

Across

1. the main part of a plant above the ground that supports the leaves and flowers; carries water to the leaves and flowers
2. the central part of a flower where the seeds are made
3. a kind of tree with leaves that fall off each autumn and grow back each spring
5. the underground part of a plant that grows down into the soil and holds the plant in place while the plant absorbs water and nutrients
7. the part of the flower's stem that holds the pollen
8. the stem part of a flower that makes pollen and is surrounded by petals

Down

1. the part of a plant that can grow into a new plant
2. the process by which plants make their own food by using energy from the sun
4. a yellowish powder found in a flower that must be carried from a stamen to a pistil in order for seeds to form
6. the part of a flower or tree that holds seeds and is usually good to eat, such as an apple or a peach

③ Word Search — Earth Science

All the words or phrases listed in the box appear in the puzzle — horizontally, vertically, diagonally, or backward. Find and circle them.

anther	seed	deciduous	pollen	roots
stamen	stem	photosynthesis	pistil	fruit

```
L I T S I P E M D N R G T O I
P U U R Q L P K E I E I B W W
H H N K M X X F C O I L T Q W
Y G O B Z A T X I C Y X L L T
N W V T N D G N D T D B O O G
T B K T O Q D K U R O O T S P
P J H V Q S N E O W N H B V E
B E Q Q G L Y E U J H V L L N
R D S W P G P N S Q V A B N T
N R C E P Z X Z T I X Z I W S
E W P H E S G I D H C L A C T
M L W Q W D U P I W E P K G E
A F K T B R I W G D U S T Z M
T E F W F S Y J J I U W I E M
S Z S Q J X N N X T R G H S E
```

100% Curriculum Vocabulary—Grades 6-12

4 Definitions — Earth Science

1. **acid rain** — rain or snow that has pollutants in it and is harmful to crops, lakes, and buildings

2. **alluvial fan** — a fan-shaped area of sand or mud where water leaves a mountain and runs into a plain

3. **catalytic converter** — a device found in cars that breaks down harmful gases in order to reduce pollution

4. **cavern** — a natural, hollow opening underground that is big enough for a person to enter

5. **crest** — the highest point of a wave

6. **delta** — a triangular pile of sand or mud that forms at the mouth of a large river

7. **desalination** — the process of removing salt from ocean water

8. **erosion** — a process by which substances are worn away by wind, rain, etc.

9. **irrigation** — the practice of supplying dry parts of land with water from another place through canals or pipes

10. **pollutant** — anything that makes the environment dirty, such as chemicals or waste

4 Fill-in-the-Blank — Earth Science

Fill in the blanks with the words or phrases from the box.

delta	cavern	catalytic converter	irrigation	acid rain
crest	desalination	alluvial fan	pollutant	erosion

1. Surfers ride a wave at its _____ because it is the highest point.

2. _____ is a process where substances are worn away by wind and rain.

3. Anything that makes the environment dirty is a _____.

4. _____ supplies dry parts of land with water from another place.

5. A device that reduces pollution is a _____.

6. A _____ is a natural, hollow opening underground.

7. The pile of sand or mud at the mouth of a river is called a _____.

8. _____ is rain or snow that has pollutants in it and is harmful to crops, lakes, and buildings.

9. _____ is the process of removing salt from ocean water.

10. An _____ is an area of sand or mud at the bottom of a mountain.

4 Word Association — Earth Science

Write the word or phrase from the box next to the word or phrase that shares a similar meaning.

delta	cavern	catalytic converter	irrigation	acid rain
crest	desalination	alluvial fan	pollutant	erosion

1. triangular pile of sand _____

2. removing salt from ocean water _____

3. underground opening _____

4. supplying with water _____

5. breaks down harmful gases _____

6. wearing away by wind or rain _____

7. rain harmful to crops and lakes _____

8. fan-shaped area of sand or mud _____

9. makes environment dirty _____

10. wave _____

4 Writing Sentences — Earth Science

Write a sentence using each word or phrase.

1. acid rain

2. alluvial fan

3. catalytic converter

4. cavern

5. crest

6. delta

7. desalination

8. erosion

9. irrigation

10. pollutant

100% Curriculum Vocabulary—Grades 6-12

Crossword Puzzle 4 — Earth Science

Complete the puzzle with words that match the clues.

Across

1. a natural, hollow opening underground that is big enough for a person to enter
5. anything that makes the environment dirty
6. the highest point of a wave
7. the practice of supplying dry parts of land with water from another place through canals or pipes
10. the process of removing salt from ocean water

Down

2. rain or snow that has pollutants in it and is harmful to crops, lakes, and buildings
3. a device found in cars that breaks down harmful gases in order to reduce pollution
4. a fan-shaped area of sand or mud where water leaves a mountain and runs into a plain
8. a process by which substances are worn away by wind, rain, etc.
9. a triangular pile of sand or mud that forms at the mouth of a large river

4 Word Search — Earth Science

All the words or phrases listed in the box appear in the puzzle — horizontally, vertically, diagonally, or backward. Find and circle them.

delta	cavern	catalytic converter	irrigation	acid rain
crest	desalination	alluvial fan	pollutant	erosion

```
S N S H K F H U N S E C V D D X A G
W L O B W J G I T Q Q A Q E T B H B
P A G I F Y A N L U W T S L N A G R
N K K S T R E J Y V X A E T A Q T H
V Q F X D A A F H O L L D A T T M M
Y F T I C V G N Z I H Y Z B U M P V
G U C R G J O I N N H T Y Z L V Z I
V A E U X Y Z A R F Z I A G L C N I
X S N J P X T J O R B C N O O U Y F
T E R O S I O N S Y I C B P P U Q S
T C I V O A T M K C N O X Z Z O U Y
U P N N K Q E L Y O A N N R R C R W
N A F L A I V U L L A V I Q W E Z E
A O I W S G F T C P C E E K G A J H
W I D D A D B K F U V R K R S E E F
F E Z H M D A X S M I T F N N Z G H
U V V N L E B G K A O E T B C T F R
E V I M O J T N Z X B R A K A X C L
```

5 Definitions — Earth Science

1. **Big Bang theory** — a theory that says a huge explosion created the universe billions of years ago

2. **Cenozoic era** — the most recent geological era that began approximately 70 million years ago when many mammals appeared, the modern continents took shape, and the glacial ice formed; often called the Ice Age

3. **earthquake** — the sudden movement of large sections of rock beneath the Earth's surface that causes shaking and trembling

4. **epicenter** — the central point of an earthquake where the strongest shaking and moving takes place

5. **glacier** — a huge mass of ice that moves slowly down a mountain or over land

6. **iceberg** — a large, floating chunk of ice that has broken off from a glacier and is in the ocean

7. **igneous rock** — a type of rock that forms from melted rock that cools and hardens; typically found under the Earth's surface or in volcanoes

8. **Mesozoic era** — the period of time from 220 to 65 million years ago when dinosaurs appeared and became extinct; often called the Age of Dinosaurs

9. **Paleozoic era** — the period of time between the Precambrian and Mesozoic eras from 600 to 220 million years ago where the first fish, amphibians, reptiles, insects, and land plants appeared

10. **Precambrian era** — the period of time ending approximately 600 million years ago when the Earth's crust was formed

5 Fill-in-the-Blank — Earth Science

Fill in the blanks with the words or phrases from the box.

| glacier | Cenozoic era | Big Bang theory | igneous rock | iceberg |
| epicenter | Paleozoic era | Precambrian era | Mesozoic era | earthquake |

1. During the _____, many mammals appeared, the modern continents took shape, and ice glaciers formed.

2. The central point of an earthquake, or the _____, is where the strongest shaking and moving takes place.

3. An _____ is the sudden movement of large sections of rock beneath the Earth's surface that causes shaking and trembling.

4. A _____ is a huge mass of ice that moves slowly down a mountain or over land.

5. The first fish, reptiles, insects, and plants appeared in the _____.

6. Some scientists believe the _____ which says a huge explosion created the universe billions of years ago.

7. _____ forms from melted rock that cools and hardens.

8. During the _____ the Earth's crust was formed.

9. A large, floating chunk of ice that has broken off from a glacier and is in the ocean is an _____.

10. The _____ is sometimes referred to as the Age of Dinosaurs.

5 Word Association — Earth Science

Write the word or phrase from the box next to the word or phrase that shares a similar meaning.

glacier	Cenozoic era	Big Bang theory	igneous rock	iceberg
epicenter	Paleozoic era	Precambrian era	Mesozoic era	earthquake

1. explosion _____

2. time when ice glaciers formed _____

3. formed from melted rock _____

4. time when fish and reptiles appeared _____

5. mass of ice in ocean _____

6. trembling of Earth's surface _____

7. time when Earth's crust formed _____

8. central point of an earthquake _____

9. mass of ice on land _____

10. time when dinosaurs appeared _____

5 Writing Sentences — EARTH SCIENCE

Write a sentence using each word or phrase.

1. Big Bang theory

2. Cenozoic era

3. earthquake

4. epicenter

5. glacier

6. iceberg

7. igneous rock

8. Mesozoic era

9. Paleozoic era

10. Precambrian era

Crossword Puzzle — Earth Science

Complete the puzzle with words that match the clues.

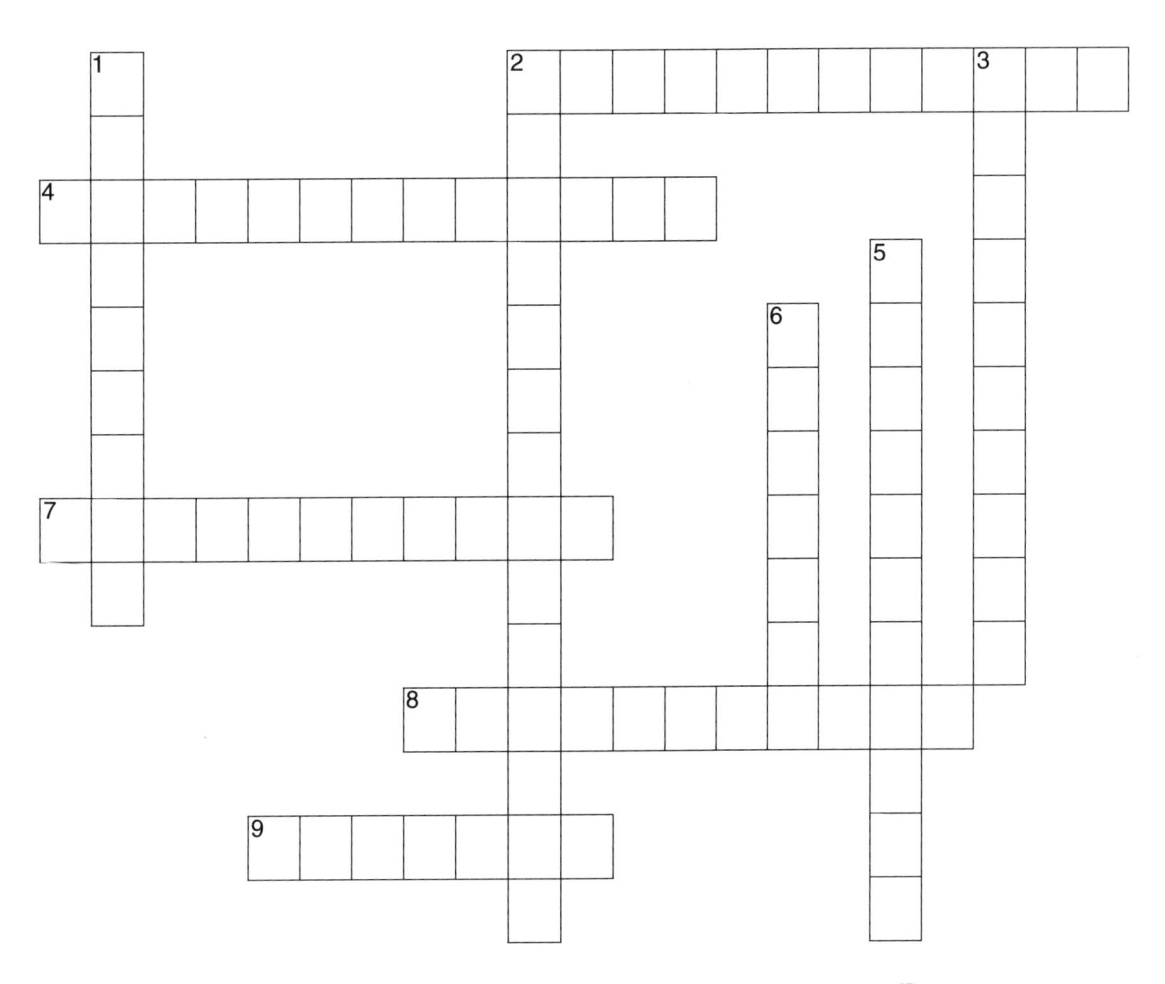

Across

2. the period of time between the Precambrian and Mesozoic eras from 600 to 220 million years ago where the first fish, amphibians, reptiles, insects, and land plants appeared
4. a theory that says a huge explosion created the universe billions of years ago
7. the most recent geological era that began 70 million years ago when many mammals appeared, the modern continents took shape, and the glacial ice formed; often called the Ice Age
8. a type of rock that forms from melted rock that cools and hardens; typically found under the Earth's surface or in volcanoes
9. a large, floating chunk of ice that has broken off from a glacier and is in the ocean

Down

1. the central point of an earthquake where the strongest shaking and moving takes place
2. the period of time ending approximately 600 million years ago when the Earth's crust was formed
3. the sudden movement of large sections of rock beneath the Earth's surface that causes shaking and trembling
5. the period of time from 220 to 65 million years ago when dinosaurs appeared and became extinct; often called the Age of Dinosaurs
6. a huge mass of ice that moves slowly down a mountain or over land

5 Word Search — Earth Science

All the words or phrases listed in the box appear in the puzzle — horizontally, vertically, diagonally, or backward. Find and circle them.

| glacier | Cenozoic era | Big Bang theory | igneous rock | iceberg |
| epicenter | Paleozoic era | Precambrian era | Mesozoic era | earthquake |

```
P R E C A M B R I A N E R A P
K A U I R K W M R V S K V B A
B X R E C K M E D A O A I Z L
R I L E J E T E Q F I U K E E
J Y G Q C N B R S G U Q U J O
G M Z B E I E E N E C H J K Z
F W P C A M O E R A M T W R O
Q M I V F N O Z C G A R I O I
U P V O D U G K O H O A Z N C
E C T Y S O T T V S W E N R E
X K N R F B Q Z H K E S G V R
K S O U B M J I H E K M W F A
G C Q A R E C I O Z O N E C B
K H L F C G L A C I E R Z F S
T C Z G S O V F I L G U Y J L
```

100% Curriculum Vocabulary—Grades 6-12

6 Definitions — Earth Science

1. **alloy** — a metal that is made by melting and mixing together two or more metals

2. **conservation** — the protection and careful use of natural resources (e.g., forest, lakes, etc) so they do not disappear

3. **contract** — to become smaller or shorter; to shrink

4. **core** — the innermost layer or center of the Earth where temperatures are nearly as hot as those on the Sun's surface

5. **data** — facts and figures that are used to draw a conclusion

6. **depletion** — the process of removing nutrients from the soil

7. **element** — a substance that is made up of just one kind of atom and cannot be broken down into any simpler substance

8. **expand** — to become larger; to grow

9. **fossil** — the imprint of a skeleton or plant on a rock or bones that is the preserved remains of a living thing

10. **fossil fuel** — fuel, such as coal, oil, and natural gas, formed from remains of dead plants and animals

6 Fill-in-the-Blank — Earth Science

Fill in the blanks with the words or phrases from the box.

alloy	contract	conservation	expand	depletion
fossil	data	fossil fuel	core	element

1. People need to practice _____ so that we can keep our forests.

2. The center of Earth is the _____.

3. Steel is an _____ because it is made up of two or more metals.

4. A _____ is the preserved remains of a living thing.

5. To become smaller is to _____.

6. An _____ is made up of just one kind of atom and cannot be broken down into any simpler substance.

7. _____ is the process of nutrients being removed from the soil.

8. _____ is formed from the remains of dead plants and animals.

9. To become larger is to _____.

10. _____ are facts and figures that is used to draw a conclusion.

6 Word Association — Earth Science

Write the word or phrase from the box next to the word or phrase that shares a similar meaning.

alloy	contract	conservation	expand	depletion
fossil	data	fossil fuel	core	element

1. facts and figures _____

2. shrink _____

3. removing nutrients from soil _____

4. coal, oil, or natural gas _____

5. one kind of atom _____

6. imprint on a rock _____

7. center _____

8. two metals _____

9. grow _____

10. use of natural resources _____

6 Writing Sentences — Earth Science

Write a sentence using each word or phrase.

1. alloy

2. conservation

3. contract

4. core

5. data

6. depletion

7. element

8. expand

9. fossil

10. fossil fuel

Crossword Puzzle — Earth Science

Complete the puzzle with words that match the clues.

Across

1. the innermost layer or center of the Earth where temperatures are nearly as hot as those on the Sun's surface
3. a substance that is made up of just one kind of atom and cannot be broken down into any simpler substance
4. fuel, such as coal, oil, and natural gas, formed from remains of dead plants and animals
6. to become smaller or shorter; to shrink
7. facts and figures that are used to draw a conclusion
8. to become larger; to grow

Down

1. the protection and careful use of natural resources (e.g., forest, lakes, etc) so they do not disappear
2. the process of removing nutrients from the soil
5. the imprint of a skeleton or plant on a rock or bones that is the preserved remains of a living thing
9. a metal that is made by melting and mixing together two or more metals

100% Curriculum Vocabulary—Grades 6-12

6 Word Search — Earth Science

All the words or phrases listed in the box appear in the puzzle — horizontally, vertically, diagonally, or backward. Find and circle them.

alloy	contract	conservation	expand	depletion
fossil	data	fossil fuel	core	element

```
D B M X Y Q Z T J N A U D I X
I A S I U G O E D K J R N P Y
J A T M N F X X E K M P A T K
F A N A N Q X J P I N C P U D
I O X T N E M E L E O X X E E
M T S Y C O R E E N Z K E B Z
C O N S E R V A T I O N J U M
F M N F I L O R I Z X J D Q Y
J E R Q Y L A L O T W E H C T
G H U R N C F L N P O O U H G
K Q X G T A D U I M C Y W P P
K C S V H G A W E S O O O D Y
J Z G K Q P R N H L S J N K I
T B X U A S Y F L L R O L J Z
E X N G L G I A O N G B F L Y
```

100% Curriculum Vocabulary—Grades 6-12

7 Definitions — Earth Science

1. **adaptation** — change in behavior or physical makeup to help living things survive in certain environments

2. **condensation** — the change that happens when water vapor (gas) turns into a liquid

3. **conduction** — the transfer of heat energy from one substance to another

4. **conifer** — a tree that bears cones and has needles instead of leaves (e.g. pine tree)

5. **elevation** — the distance or height of the land above the sea or ocean

6. **equator** — an imaginary horizontal line around the middle of the Earth that divides the northern and southern hemispheres

7. **front** — the place where two different air masses with different temperatures meet and usually cause a change in the weather

8. **hazardous waste** — products or garbage that can harm human health or the environment if handled improperly; also called *toxic waste*

9. **hemisphere** — one half of the Earth; either northern/southern or eastern/western

10. **quasar** — a star-like object that sends out powerful radio waves or bright light

7 Fill-in-the-Blank — Earth Science

Fill in the blanks with the words or phrases from the box.

conifer	quasar	hazardous waste	conduction	elevation
front	equator	condensation	hemisphere	adaptation

1. How high a city is above sea level is its _____.

2. _____ is a product or dangerous garbage that can harm human health or the environment if handled improperly.

3. A change in the weather can be caused by a _____.

4. A _____ is a star-like object that sends out powerful radio waves.

5. An imaginary line around the middle of Earth is the _____.

6. _____ is change in behavior or physical makeup that helps living things to survive in certain environments.

7. The northern half of the Earth is the northern _____.

8. _____ occurs when water vapor changes to a liquid.

9. A tree that has needles instead of leaves and bears cones is a _____.

10. The transfer of heat energy from one substance to another is _____.

7 Word Association — Earth Science

Write the word or phrase from the box next to the word or phrase that shares a similar meaning.

conifer	quasar	hazardous waste	conduction	elevation
front	equator	condensation	hemisphere	adaptation

1. causes weather change _____

2. height _____

3. star-like object _____

4. dangerous garbage _____

5. pine tree _____

6. change to survive environment _____

7. imaginary line around Earth _____

8. one half of the Earth _____

9. energy transfer _____

10. gas to liquid _____

7 Writing Sentences — EARTH SCIENCE

Write a sentence using each word or phrase.

1. adaptation

2. condensation

3. conduction

4. conifer

5. elevation

6. equator

7. front

8. hazardous waste

9. hemisphere

10. quasar

100% Curriculum Vocabulary—Grades 6-12

7 Crossword Puzzle — Earth Science

Complete the puzzle with words that match the clues.

Across

3. a star-like object that sends out powerful radio waves or bright light
7. an imaginary horizontal line around the middle of the Earth
8. products or garbage that can harm human health or the environment if handled improperly
9. a tree that bears cones and has needles instead of leaves (e.g. pine tree)
10. the place where two different air masses with different temperatures meet and usually cause a change in the weather

Down

1. one half of the Earth; either northern/southern or eastern/western
2. the change that happens when water vapor (gas) turns into a liquid
4. change in behavior or physical makeup to help living things survive in certain environments
5. the distance or height of the land above the sea or ocean
6. the transfer of heat energy from one substance to another

100% Curriculum Vocabulary—Grades 6-12   125   Copyright © 2002 LinguiSystems, Inc.

⑦ Word Search — Earth Science

All the words or phrases listed in the box appear in the puzzle — horizontally, vertically, diagonally, or backward. Find and circle them.

conifer	quasar	hazardous waste	conduction	elevation
front	equator	condensation	hemisphere	adaptation

```
L N Y E S I F P W V A L X H N
J L F R X U V E Q M S D A M O
L N Y N G U L U I B C Z R N I
T N O R F E A C H F A C Z E T
O J Y X V S R U O R E N V Q A
N O I T A S N E D N O C R U T
S D E R D K X O H I I M N A P
P S G B U V U V T P R F B T A
U Z D B A S W C E G S T E O D
Z H B I W Q U K J N T I C R A
J K N A V D O E P M W L M Q K
J N S U N D Z J O D J J C E Z
L T P O E L E V A T I O N O H
E N C O G O S Q K H B W W P G
E M I V R N X K K J J W J Q N
```

① Definitions — English

1. **abbreviation** — a shortened form of a word or phrase used in place of the whole word; often followed by a period (e.g., Doctor = Dr.)

2. **apostrophe (')** — a punctuation mark used in a possessive (e.g., Maria's pen) or in a contraction (e.g., don't)

3. **capitalize** — to make the first letter of a word an uppercase letter

4. **colon (:)** — a punctuation mark used before a list of items; before a long, formal statement or quotation; or between an hour and a minute (e.g., 6:30)

5. **comma (,)** — a punctuation mark used to separate things in a series or words in days and months (e.g., Saturday, May 19)

6. **contraction** — a word formed by putting two words together replacing one or two letters with an apostrophe (e.g., do not = don't)

7. **end marks** — punctuation marks used at the end of a sentence: a period (.), question mark (?), and exclamation point (!)

8. **proofread** — to read over a piece of writing before it is finished in order to find and correct any mistakes

9. **quotation (" ") marks** — punctuation marks used to enclose a person's exact words (e.g., Kelly said, "Hi.")

10. **semicolon (;)** — a punctuation mark used between independent clauses if they are not joined by words like *but*, *or*, and *and*; a mark used between words in a series if they contain commas (e.g., Chicago, IL; Phoenix, AZ)

100% Curriculum Vocabulary—Grades 6-12

1 Fill-in-the-Blank — English

Fill in the blanks with the words or phrases from the box.

semicolon	colon	quotation marks	end marks	capitalize
proofread	comma	abbreviation	contraction	apostrophe

1. An _____ is a mark used in a possessive or in a contraction.

2. To separate things in a series, use a _____.

3. When writing, you _____ the first letter of a sentence.

4. *Don't* is a _____ of the words *do* and *not*.

5. A _____ is a punctuation mark used between independent clauses and between words in a series if they contain commas.

6. The marks used to enclose a person's exact words are _____.

7. Periods, question marks, and exclamation points are all called _____.

8. An _____ is a shortened form used in place of the whole word.

9. A _____ is used before a list of items or between an hour and a minute.

10. When you _____, you read over a piece of writing in order to find and correct any mistakes that it may have.

100% Curriculum Vocabulary—Grades 6-12

1. Word Association — English

Write the word or phrase from the box next to the word or phrase that shares a similar meaning.

> semicolon   colon   quotation marks   end marks   capitalize
>
> proofread   comma   abbreviation   contraction   apostrophe

1. *can't* _____

2. used in a contraction _____

3. mark errors _____

4. to begin with an uppercase letter _____

5. . ? ! _____

6. goes before a list of items _____

7. *Dr.* _____

8. encloses exact words _____

9. used to separate things in a list _____

10. used with independent clauses _____

① Writing Sentences — English

Write a sentence using each word or phrase.

1. abbreviation

2. apostrophe

3. capitalize

4. colon

5. comma

6. contraction

7. end marks

8. proofread

9. quotation marks

10. semicolon

Crossword Puzzle — English

Complete the puzzle with words that match the clues.

Across

3. a punctuation mark used in a possessive or in a contraction
5. to read over a piece of writing before it's finished in order to find and correct any mistakes
6. punctuation marks used to enclose a person's exact words
7. to make the first letter of a word an uppercase letter
8. a punctuation mark used before a list of items; before a long, formal statement or quotation; or between an hour and a minute

Down

1. a word formed by putting together two words replacing one or two letters with an apostrophe
2. a punctuation mark used between independent clauses if they are not joined by words like *but*, *or*, and *and*; a mark used between words in a series if they contain commas
3. a shortened form of a word or phrase used in place of the whole word; often followed by a period
4. punctuation marks used at the end of a sentence
7. a punctuation mark used to separate things in a series or words in days and months

1 Word Search — English

All the words or phrases listed in the box appear in the puzzle — horizontally, vertically, diagonally, or backward. Find and circle them.

| semicolon | colon | quotation marks | end marks | capitalize |
| proofread | comma | abbreviation | contraction | apostrophe |

```
Q O E N D M A R K S C F W K C
E U R F A I B N Y J B O M D C
X F O V R S B Z H J U O L O D
B E C T N Y R Z R Z H C N O D
J Y Z Z A K E H C S P T S C N
I H G I A T V F X X R Z W L W
J Z N U L L I P L A A D T D N
R I C C E A A O C S W E A G O
S D O U M B T T N M Y E S N L
T E M D F D I I Y M R E G K O
D X M H C O O B P F A I Q J C
J I A H N U N J O A Q R O N I
E H P O R T S O P A C T K C M
O P I D N U R B P L E L T S E
F Q E M P P A U X X T W A O S
```

100% Curriculum Vocabulary—Grades 6-12

2 Definitions — English

1. **adjective** — a word used to describe a noun or pronoun

2. **adverb** — a word used to describe a verb, an adjective, or another adverb

3. **comparative** — a word used to compare two things

4. **metaphor** — a comparison of two very different things to show how they are alike without using the words *like* or *as* (e.g., A blanket of snow fell through the night.)

5. **noun** — a word used to name a person, place, thing, or idea

6. **pronoun** — a word that takes the place of a noun to refer to a person, place, or thing

7. **proper noun** — a noun that names one person, place, or thing and is spelled with a capital letter

8. **simile** — a comparison of two very different things to show how they are alike using the words *like* or *as* (e.g., He is as tough as nails.)

9. **superlative** — a word used to compare more than two things or the highest level of comparison (e.g., She is the tallest girl in her class.)

10. **verb** — a word used to describe an action or to help make a statement

2 Fill-in-the-Blank — English

Fill in the blanks with the words or phrases from the box.

noun	pronoun	superlative	adverb	metaphor
verb	adjective	comparative	simile	proper noun

1. A _____ is a word used to describe an action or to help make a statement.

2. The highest degree of comparison is a _____.

3. An _____ is a word used to describe a noun or pronoun.

4. A word used to name a person, place, thing, or idea is a _____.

5. A _____ is a comparison of two very different things using the words *like* or *as*.

6. An _____ is a word used to describe a verb, adjective, or another adverb.

7. A _____ names one person, place, or thing and begins with a capital letter.

8. A word used to compare two things is a _____.

9. A _____ refers to a person, place, or thing and takes the place of a noun.

10. A _____ is a comparison of two very different things without using the words *like* or *as*.

② Word Association — English

Write the word or phrase from the box next to the word or phrase that shares a similar meaning.

noun	pronoun	superlative	adverb	metaphor
verb	adjective	comparative	simile	proper noun

1. comparison with *like* or *as* _____

2. action word _____

3. takes the place of a noun _____

4. highest comparison _____

5. person, place, thing, or idea _____

6. describes a verb _____

7. comparison without *like* or *as* _____

8. describes a noun _____

9. a noun with a capital letter _____

10. compares two things _____

② Writing Sentences — English

Write a sentence using each word or phrase.

1. adjective

2. adverb

3. comparative

4. metaphor

5. noun

6. pronoun

7. proper noun

8. simile

9. superlative

10. verb

Crossword Puzzle — English

Complete the puzzle with words that match the clues.

Across

4. a word that takes the place of a noun to refer to a person, place, or thing
6. a word used to describe a noun or pronoun
7. a word used to name a person, place, thing, or idea
8. a comparison of two very different things to show how they are alike without using the words *like* or *as*
9. a comparison of two very different things to show how they are alike using the words *like* or *as*
10. a word used to compare two things

Down

1. a word used to describe an action or to help make a statement
2. a word used to compare more than two things or the highest level of comparison
3. a word used to describe a verb, an adjective, or another adverb
5. a noun that names one person, place, or thing and is spelled with a capital letter

② Word Search — English

All the words or phrases listed in the box appear in the puzzle — horizontally, vertically, diagonally, or backward. Find and circle them.

noun	pronoun	superlative	adverb	metaphor
verb	adjective	comparative	simile	proper noun

```
X J A D A T T N N P Q E C Z A
Z Z R H E M A V R O Z C L Z R
Z J Y U L M E O Q S U Y J N N
P A E G L T P O B U T N D U E
C C Z J G E S R P P E Y N O Z
X O K S R A E D R E Y J K N N
R U M N U V M M N R A P C O E
Q O O P D S I M I L E G S R S
G U H A A Y B P B A O V N P O
N I J P J R E V I T C E J D A
Q R C I A J A W M I M R K R R
G D I I W T X T M V Q B U C P
S O R D J B E C I E L V O D S
Y O H C Q K F M D V L O N O M
R T G N M S I M K A E R Y Q R
```

3 Definitions — English

1. **conclusion** — the ending or last paragraph in a written work

2. **context** — words in a sentence or paragraph that surround a word and help a person understand the meaning of that word

3. **diagram** — a drawing or plan that explains something by showing all its parts, how it is put together, or how it works

4. **draft** — a rough copy or a plan for a piece of writing

5. **idea** — a belief, plan, or picture in the mind; a thought or an opinion

6. **main idea** — the most important idea in a paragraph

7. **order** — the way things are placed or the sequence of something

8. **paragraph** — a group of sentences that relate to a main idea; a piece of writing starting on a new line and usually indented from the other lines

9. **plagiarism** — using someone else's ideas or words as if they were your own

10. **topic** — a subject that people think, write, or talk about

3 Fill-in-the-Blank — English

Fill in the blanks with the words or phrases from the box.

idea	topic	plagiarism	paragraph	main idea
draft	context	conclusion	order	diagram

1. A subject, or _____, is something that people think or talk about.

2. The most important idea of a paragraph is the _____.

3. Use the _____ of the sentence to help you understand the words.

4. The _____ is the ending or last paragraph in a written work.

5. A plan for a piece of writing is a _____.

6. A _____ is a group of sentences that relate to a main idea.

7. An _____ is a belief, plan, or picture in someone's mind.

8. _____ is using someone else's ideas or words as if they were your own.

9. The _____ of something is the way it is placed or its sequence.

10. When putting something together, it helps to have a _____ that shows all the parts and how they work.

3 Word Association — English

Write the word or phrase from the box next to the word or phrase that shares a similar meaning.

> idea   topic   plagiarism   paragraph   main idea
> draft   context   conclusion   order   diagram

1. surrounding words in a sentence _____

2. last paragraph _____

3. using someone else's words _____

4. most important idea in a paragraph _____

5. group of sentences _____

6. drawing _____

7. subject _____

8. sequence _____

9. rough copy _____

10. belief _____

3. Writing Sentences — English

Write a sentence using each word or phrase.

1. conclusion

2. context

3. diagram

4. draft

5. idea

6. main idea

7. order

8. paragraph

9. plagiarism

10. topic

Crossword Puzzle — English

Complete the puzzle with words that match the clues.

Across

4. a drawing or plan that explains something by showing all its parts, how it is put together, or how it works
5. using someone else's ideas or words as if they were your own
7. a rough copy or a plan for a piece of writing
9. the way things are placed or the sequence of something
10. a belief, plan, or picture in the mind; a thought or an opinion

Down

1. the ending or last paragraph in a written work
2. a group of sentences that relate to a main idea
3. the most important idea in a paragraph
6. words in a sentence or paragraph that surround a word and help a person understand the meaning of that word
8. a subject that people think, write, or talk about

3 Word Search — English

All the words or phrases listed in the box appear in the puzzle — horizontally, vertically, diagonally, or backward. Find and circle them.

idea	topic	plagiarism	paragraph	main idea
draft	context	conclusion	order	diagram

```
N I D I D R B Z D H M E E U J
B O C I P O T I P A S J X S U
T Z I E A T B A X E I W F E L
T F H S E G R K K D R Z L M O
O V A M U G R Q L I A E R O I
T K D R A L M A I N I D E A J
N X P R D N C T M H G G J A B
N C A G L K O N C N A C Q V R
Z P U V K T C L O O L O C H V
N L R Q M P M O R C P N W C F
W M Y Y J L A D X X S T V W E
U G F T O R E R F T O E C X B
X O K C E R Q V I N Z X V B B
H K E P F I R M S M P T U S X
J R W K D X S G M B X J N G U
```

100% Curriculum Vocabulary—Grades 6-12 Copyright © 2002 LinguiSystems, Inc.

4 Definitions — English

1. **analogy** — a comparison of two unlike things to show how their characteristics are alike (e.g., the branches of a tree are like the branches of a river)

2. **anecdote** — a very short story about something that happened

3. **anonymous** — from or by a person whose name is not known or is not given

4. **author** — a person who writes a book, story, or similar work

5. **character** — a person or animal in a story

6. **idiom** — a group of words that do not carry their usual meaning but go together to create an expression with a special meaning (e.g., David is in the doghouse = David is in trouble.)

7. **myth** — a story that attempts to explain something that happens in life or in nature, or explain about religious beliefs or the supernatural

8. **nonfiction** — writing that tells about real people, places, or events

9. **persuasion** — a type of writing in which the author tries to convince the reader to think or act in a certain way

10. **plot** — the group of events that happen in order to solve the problem or conflict in a story; the story line

4 Fill-in-the-Blank — English

Fill in the blanks with the words from the box.

| analogy | myth | character | anonymous | persuasion |
| author | anecdote | nonfiction | idiom | plot |

1. When the author of a book is unknown, he or she is _____.

2. _____ writing tells about real people, places, or events.

3. The story line, or _____ of a story, is the group of events that happen.

4. A _____ can be a person or an animal in a story.

5. An _____ is a comparison of two unlike things to show how their characteristics are alike.

6. A very short story telling about something that has happened is an _____.

7. A type of writing that tries to convince the reader to think or act in a way that the author wants is called _____.

8. An example of an _____ is "It's raining cats and dogs."

9. An _____ is a person who writes a book, story, or similar work.

10. A _____ is a story that attempts to explain something that happens in life or in nature, or explain about religious beliefs or the supernatural.

100% Curriculum Vocabulary—Grades 6-12

4 Word Association — English

Write the word from the box next to the word or phrase that shares a similar meaning.

> analogy   myth   character   anonymous   persuasion
> author   anecdote   nonfiction   idiom   plot

1. story that explains something _____
2. very short story _____
3. person in a story _____
4. no name given _____
5. writer _____
6. writing about real events _____
7. an expression with a special meaning _____
8. comparison of two unlike things _____
9. story line _____
10. type of writing to convince _____

4 Writing Sentences — English

Write a sentence using each word.

1. analogy

2. anecdote

3. anonymous

4. author

5. character

6. idiom

7. myth

8. nonfiction

9. persuasion

10. plot

4 Crossword Puzzle — English

Complete the puzzle with words that match the clues.

Across

1. the story line or group of events that happen in a story
4. a very short story telling about something that happened
5. a comparison of two unlike things to show how their characteristics are alike
6. a group of words that do not carry their usual meaning but go together to create an expression with a special meaning
7. writing that tells about real people, places, or events
8. a person who writes a book

Down

1. a type of writing in which the author tries to convince the reader to think or act in a certain way
2. a story that attempts to explain something that happens in life or in nature
3. a person written about in a story
4. from or by a person whose name is not known or is not given

④ Word Search — English

All the words or phrases listed in the box appear in the puzzle — horizontally, vertically, diagonally, or backward. Find and circle them.

analogy	myth	character	anonymous	persuasion
author	anecdote	nonfiction	idiom	plot

```
M R C P B P B R J K V X C E Q
D Y J Z R C O J C G C A H N D
K Y T Q K N B E K Y U L A S C
P J G H T T Y B E S G N R K I
J E N O N F I C T I O N A D S
Y E R V L J T R W N W V C V L
D C H S R A Y O Y E F X T G X
Z E Z H U M N M B A S F E N F
J R I L W A O A R U S H R B B
Y X S B O U S K G H R M M G H
R C E K S X W I A Y O R T U M
R G C C F N R N O I H T R D R
E T O D C E N A D N T D N C J
G L P M H L O I B P U R P X J
Z H H D P L O T V F A D A M V
```

100% Curriculum Vocabulary—Grades 6-12

5 Definitions — English

1. **accept** — to receive or take something that is offered or given to you

2. **among** — one of many things (use when you are writing about a group of things or more than two things [e.g., She was *among* her friends.])

3. **between** — shared by (use when you are writing about two things at a time [e.g., This is *between* you and me.])

4. **clarify** — to make something clearer or easier to understand

5. **except** — not including someone or something (e.g., Everyone went to lunch *except* Ramon.)

6. **explanation** — words that explain something that happened or that make the meaning of something clearer

7. **fact** — a statement that can be proven true

8. **instruction** — direction on how to do something

9. **mediate** — to settle an argument or fight by bringing the two parties or people together and talking about the problem

10. **opinion** — the way someone feels about something; a statement that cannot be proven true or false

5 Fill-in-the-Blank — English

Fill in the blanks with the words from the box.

accept	opinion	clarify	instruction	mediate
between	fact	explanation	among	except

1. An _____ is a way to explain something that happened.

2. You use the word _____ when you are writing about two things at a time.

3. Every month has at least 30 days _____ February.

4. To _____ is to make something clearer or easier to understand.

5. To _____ something is to take what is offered or given to you.

6. An _____ is the way someone feels about something.

7. A statement that can be proven true is a _____.

8. You use the word _____ when you are writing about a group of things or more than two things.

9. To settle a fight, people can _____.

10. Direction on how to do something is an _____.

5 Word Association — English

Write the word from the box next to the word or phrase that shares a similar meaning.

accept	opinion	clarify	instruction	mediate
between	fact	explanation	among	except

1. not include something or someone _____

2. shared by _____

3. proven true _____

4. settle an argument _____

5. direction _____

6. to receive _____

7. words that explain _____

8. make something clearer _____

9. one of many things _____

10. not true or false _____

100% Curriculum Vocabulary—Grades 6-12

5 Writing Sentences — English

Write a sentence using each word.

1. accept

2. among

3. between

4. clarify

5. except

6. explanation

7. fact

8. instruction

9. mediate

10. opinion

Crossword Puzzle — English

Complete the puzzle with words that match the clues.

Across

1. a statement that can be proven true
5. words that explain something that happened or that make the meaning of something clearer
6. to make something clearer or easier to understand
7. shared by
9. the way someone feels about something; a statement that cannot be proven true or false
10. to receive or take something that is offered or given to you

Down

2. one of many things
3. to settle an argument or fight by bringing the two parties or people together and talking about the problem
4. direction on how to do something
8. not including someone or something

5 Word Search — English

All the words or phrases listed in the box appear in the puzzle — horizontally, vertically, diagonally, or backward. Find and circle them.

accept	opinion	clarify	instruction	mediate
between	fact	explanation	among	except

```
V C U T U S X L M T J P N N E
Q O L P P E X E D Z D O W X C
U D M A M E D O K I I Z Z R D
A T T A R I C K S T M A C G F
B C H M A I I C A Q M V U X V
E Q G T L U F N A H U E R U I
T U E K Y X A Y K W T F N J U
W Y Y P G L U H D S P W A J W
E Q B N P J Q P T U E Z T X V
E W O X I N S T R U C T I O N
N M E L I L R I T B X I W R S
A H U V Y F A C T Y E J P H
N O I N I P O I A F V P V G R
L M C Z L Y N O I A P S A O I
O L Q F E I A H L D A G V N N
```

100% Curriculum Vocabulary—Grades 6-12

6 Definitions — English

1. **dictionary** — a book that lists words in alphabetical order and gives their meanings, pronunciation, and other information

2. **principal** — a person who is in charge of a school

3. **principle** — a rule, truth, or belief that forms the basis of other rules, truths, or beliefs

4. **than** — a word that is used to compare two or more things
   (e.g., John is taller *than* Anton.)

5. **their** — a pronoun used to show ownership by two or more people
   (e.g., *Their* cat's name is Fluffy.)

6. **then** — a word used to tell that something is happening at a certain time or soon afterward (e.g., He put on his coat and *then* he left.)

7. **there** — a word that means a general location
   (e.g., *There* is a grocery store on Pleasant Street.)

8. **they're** — the contraction of the words *they are* (e.g., *They're* sisters.)

9. **you're** — the contraction of the words *you are* (e.g., *You're* 14 years old.)

10. **your** — the possessive word for *you* (e.g., That is *your* dog.)

6 Fill-in-the-Blank — English

Fill in the blanks with the words from the box.

dictionary	principal	then	their	they're
there	you're	than	your	principle

1. _____ is a word that means a general location.

2. A word that shows ownership by two or more people is _____.

3. An adverb used to describe something happening at a certain time is _____.

4. A word used to compare two things is _____.

5. The possessive of *you* is _____.

6. A _____ is a book that lists words in alphabetical order and gives their meanings, pronunciation, and other information.

7. The person who is in charge of a school is the _____.

8. The contraction of *they are* is _____.

9. A _____ is a rule, truth, or belief that forms the basis of other rules, truths, or beliefs.

10. The contraction for *you are* is _____.

6 Word Association — English

Write the word from the box next to the word or phrase that shares a similar meaning.

> dictionary   principal   then   their   they're
> there   you're   than   your   principle

1. pronoun used to show ownership by more than one person   _____

2. contraction for *you are*   _____

3. possessive of *you*   _____

4. word used to compare   _____

5. person in charge   _____

6. rule or truth   _____

7. general location   _____

8. contraction for *they are*   _____

9. word used to show time   _____

10. book of words   _____

6 Writing Sentences — English

Write a sentence using each word.

1. dictionary

2. principal

3. principle

4. than

5. their

6. then

7. there

8. they're

9. you're

10. your

6 Crossword Puzzle — English

Complete the puzzle with words that match the clues.

Across

1. a word used to tell that something is happening at a certain time or soon afterward
4. a rule, truth, or belief that forms the basis of other rules, truths, or beliefs
8. a book that lists words and their meanings

Down

1. a contraction of the words *they are*
2. a contraction of the words *you are*
3. a word that is used to compare two or more things
5. a person who is in charge of a school
6. a pronoun that shows ownership by two or more people
7. the possessive word for *you*
9. a word that means a general location

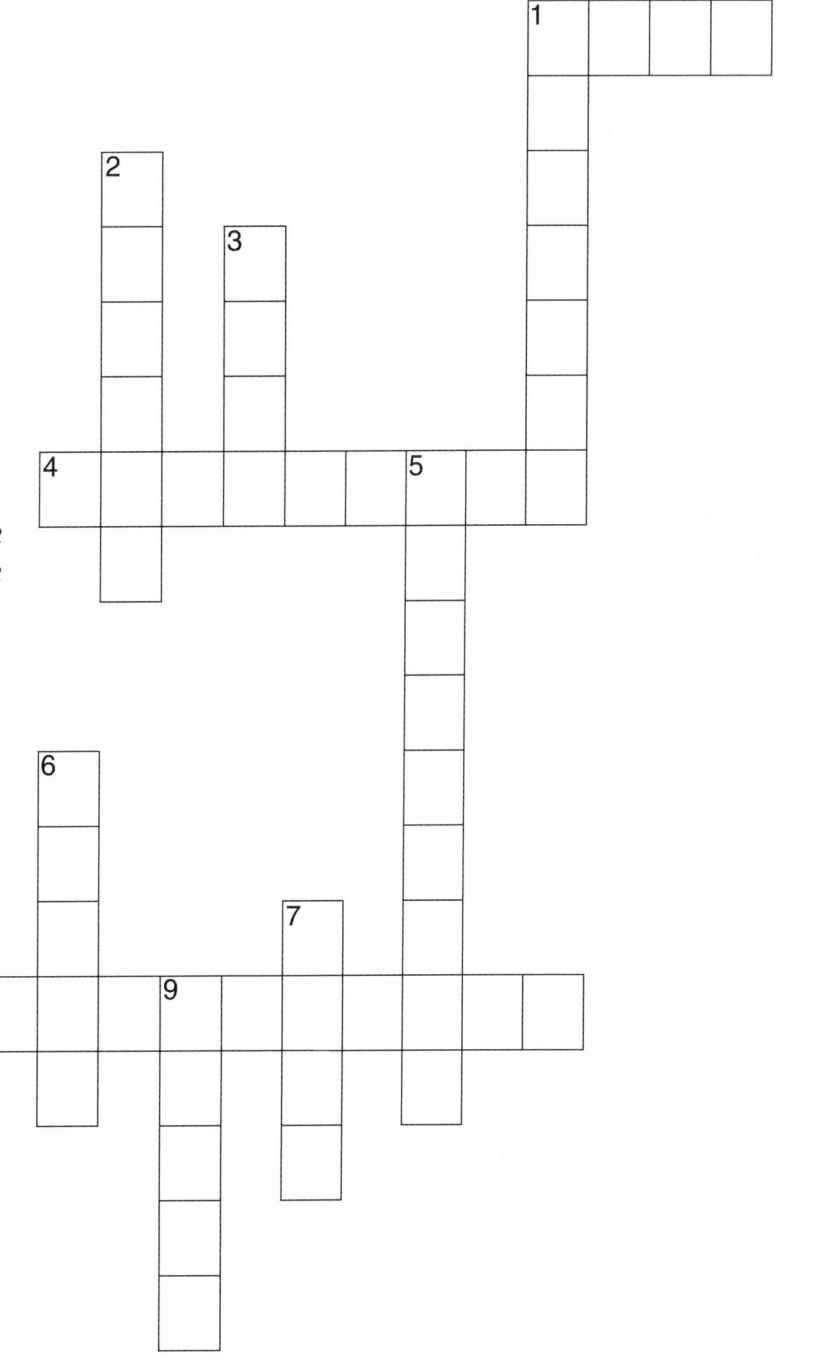

6 Word Search — English

All the words or phrases listed in the box appear in the puzzle — horizontally, vertically, diagonally, or backward. Find and circle them.

dictionary	principal	then	their	they're
there	you're	than	your	principle

```
P D J L T X G Q J Z D T B A I
O I M A L Y I T C C E S D S C
I C Q P D A E O E D U R D Q F
C T V I C K C O R Y E G E E Q
L I U C B C H X ' N J R Q H S
T O C N A C G S Y B L B Y L T
I N T I N E H T E H N D H W Q
M A L R I R H N H Y T U D U F
K R L P O A X M T E E V W Y M
G Y O X P W D M I V D B A O Y
R J M H K P R I N C I P L E O
T H E I R Y P W B N C A X I U
C A F T X U O R T H A N G C '
I Y A G U C H U Q D V C K T R
Y U Q P G X P N R F Q P Z A E
```

100% Curriculum Vocabulary—Grades 6-12

7 Definitions — English

1. **autobiography** — a book written by someone about his own life

2. **clause** — a group of words with a subject and a verb that is used as part of a sentence

3. **dependent clause (subordinate)** — a clause with a subject and verb that does not express a complete thought and cannot stand alone as a sentence

4. **description** — a group of details given to help the reader or listener imagine a person, place, object, or event

5. **detail** — a specific example that makes the meaning of a word or story clearer

6. **double negative** — the use of two negative words when only one is needed (e.g., I *don't* have *no* food.)

7. **encyclopedia** — a book or set of books that gives information about many things

8. **independent clause (main)** — a clause with a subject and verb that expresses a complete thought and can stand alone as a sentence

9. **phrase** — two or more words that go together to make an idea but do not have a subject and a verb and cannot stand alone as a sentence

10. **statement** — something that is expressed in words

7 Fill-in-the-Blank — English

Fill in the blanks with the words or phrases from the box.

autobiography	independent clause	detail	double negative	dependent clause
description	clause	encyclopedia	phrase	statement

1. A clause that has a subject and a verb and expresses a complete thought is an _____.

2. A _____ is two or more words that go together to make an idea but cannot stand alone as a sentence.

3. A _____ is a group of words that has a subject and a verb.

4. The _____ of something is a group of details that help you imagine a person, place, object, or event.

5. A _____ is a specific example that makes the meaning of a word or story clearer.

6. A _____ is something that is expressed in words.

7. A clause with a subject and a verb that doesn't express a complete thought is a _____.

8. If a person writes a book about himself, it is an _____.

9. A _____ is the use of two negative words when only one is needed.

10. A book or set of books that gives information is an _____.

100% Curriculum Vocabulary—Grades 6-12 Copyright © 2002 LinguiSystems, Inc.

7 Word Association — English

Write the word or phrase from the box next to the word or phrase that shares a similar meaning.

autobiography	independent clause	detail	double negative	dependent clause
description	clause	encyclopedia	phrase	statement

1. specific example _____

2. clause that expresses a complete thought _____

3. sentence _____

4. group of words with a subject and a verb _____

5. two negative words _____

6. clause that doesn't express a complete thought _____

7. set of books _____

8. no subject or verb _____

9. book about own life _____

10. group of details _____

100% Curriculum Vocabulary—Grades 6-12   Copyright © 2002 LinguiSystems, Inc.

7 Writing Sentences — English

Write a sentence using each word or phrase.

1. autobiography _____

2. clause _____

3. dependent clause _____

4. description _____

5. detail _____

6. double negative _____

7. encyclopedia _____

8. independent clause _____

9. phrase _____

10. statement _____

Crossword Puzzle 7 — English

Complete the puzzle with words that match the clues.

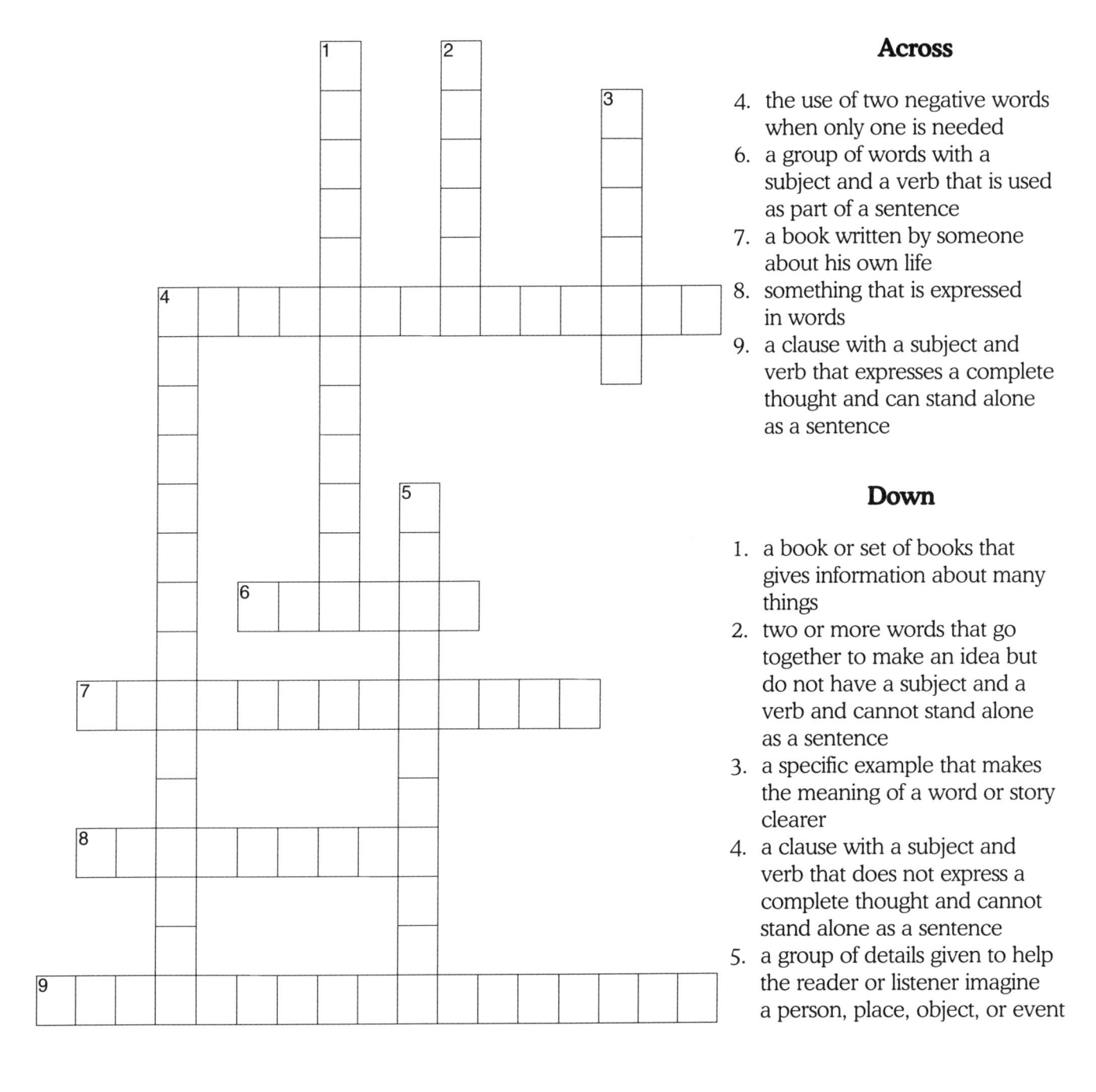

Across

4. the use of two negative words when only one is needed
6. a group of words with a subject and a verb that is used as part of a sentence
7. a book written by someone about his own life
8. something that is expressed in words
9. a clause with a subject and verb that expresses a complete thought and can stand alone as a sentence

Down

1. a book or set of books that gives information about many things
2. two or more words that go together to make an idea but do not have a subject and a verb and cannot stand alone as a sentence
3. a specific example that makes the meaning of a word or story clearer
4. a clause with a subject and verb that does not express a complete thought and cannot stand alone as a sentence
5. a group of details given to help the reader or listener imagine a person, place, object, or event

7 Word Search — English

All the words or phrases listed in the box appear in the puzzle — horizontally, vertically, diagonally, or backward. Find and circle them.

| autobiography | independent clause | detail | double negative | dependent clause |
| description | clause | encyclopedia | phrase | statement |

```
E U Z H C F F H J U L X S G T A I
V V Q F I O F N M X U B J E I N R
S F I F Z G X X U Q U Q Z D D B U
V T R T S W U I P G Y U E E Q T O
T P A H A G C H M X Q P P L C J N
Z B U T C G R O B X O E X B Y Z D
E S C A E A E I B L N H X A H E W
Y W L C S M T N C D B W F F P L U
K T A E K U E Y E J Q W J E A S H
B J U R Y W C N J L V J H H R X C
I G S H Q N T B T I B K J Y G A U
H B E C E C J Y Q F O U S I O G J
X F W Z L I A T E D V E O F I S N
V N N A D Q J J V F B D E D B K Z
X D U D E S C R I P T I O N O C N
N S X M M R X I K K D N T B T M R
E N R Z E S T W J D V E G F U Q M
J W C D Z C Q H X S Y D G E A G K
Z O A Y J O X U G Y B T K J I Q Y
E S U A L C T N E D N E P E D O T
```

100% Curriculum Vocabulary—Grades 6-12 Copyright © 2002 LinguiSystems, Inc.

① Definitions — Government

1. **boycott** — refusing to buy or sell something as a way of protesting and/or forcing a change

2. **deficit** — an amount by which there is less of something than is needed

3. **document** — an official paper than contains important information

4. **economy** — how a country supports its people through the buying and selling of goods and services

5. **excise tax** — a tax on the production, sale, or use of goods made and used within a country

6. **free enterprise** — an economic system in which businesses can operate without the government interfering

7. **loss** — a business term that describes the amount by which money paid out during a certain time is greater than money taken in

8. **profit** — a business term that describes the amount of money a company has after all bills are paid

9. **surplus** — an extra amount of something

10. **tariff** — a tax charged on goods brought into or out of a country

1 Fill-in-the-Blank — Government

Fill in the blanks with the words or phrases from the box.

surplus	profit	tariff	economy	document
excise tax	loss	deficit	boycott	free enterprise

1. A _____ is people refusing to buy or sell something as a way of protesting and/or forcing a change.

2. A _____ is an amount by which there is less of something than is needed.

3. An official paper is called a _____.

4. An _____ is how a country supports its people through the buying and selling of goods and services.

5. A tax on goods made and used in a country is an _____.

6. Businesses can operate the way they want to because of _____.

7. In a business, a _____ is the amount by which money paid out is greater than money taken in.

8. A _____ is the amount of money a company has after all bills are paid.

9. An extra amount of something is a _____.

10. A _____ is a tax charged on goods brought into or out of a country.

1 Word Association — Government

Write the word or phrase from the box next to the word or phrase that shares a similar meaning.

| boycott | document | excise tax | loss | surplus |
| deficit | economy | free enterprise | profit | tariff |

1. businesses operating independently _____

2. refusal to buy or sell _____

3. extra amount of something _____

4. gain _____

5. less of something _____

6. buying and selling goods and services _____

7. official paper _____

8. lose money _____

9. tax on goods brought into a country _____

10. tax on goods made and used in a country _____

1 Writing Sentences — Government

Write a sentence using each word or phrase.

1. boycott

2. deficit

3. document

4. economy

5. excise tax

6. free enterprise

7. loss

8. profit

9. surplus

10. tariff

Crossword Puzzle — Government

Complete the puzzle with words that match the clues.

Across

5. an amount by which there is less of something than is needed
6. an official paper than contains important information
8. the amount by which money paid out during a certain time is greater than money taken in
10. a system where businesses can operate without the government interfering

Down

1. a tax charged on goods brought into or out of a country
2. the amount of money a company has after all bills are paid
3. people refusing to buy or sell something as a way of protesting and/or forcing a change
4. the way a country provides and uses goods and services
7. a tax on the production, sale, or use of goods made and used within a country
9. an extra amount of something

1 Word Search — Government

All the words or phrases listed in the box appear in the puzzle — horizontally, vertically, diagonally, or backward. Find and circle them.

boycott	free enterprise	excise tax	document	surplus
economy	deficit	profit	loss	tariff

```
E R J X U J U T I U W H E S N
D S F S M Q N T I F O R P S Z
L P I X U E L E E G Q M M O I
H E V R M R S I T F J X E L A
F F L U P E P Z I B N A M I S
F D C P F R H L H L F T D C E
C O S S C F E C U L O E E A N
D W I Q C K I T F S R S F F J
R R I A C O B R N I E I I I X
K X O E Z O K N A E G C C C F
V K U T Y O I Y Y T E X I I I
H D G C C Q M L J L C E T O F
O C O U D G G Z S J L X R O B
Y T E C O N O M Y C G I D F P
T T F P C X Z C M H P H G I E
```

100% Curriculum Vocabulary—Grades 6–12

② Definitions — Government

1. **Congress** — the lawmaking body of the United States government; made up of two groups of people: the Senate and the House of Representatives

2. **consent** — to give permission; agree to

3. **democracy** — a form of government in which people (voters) make political decisions by voting

4. **executive branch** — the part of the government that carries out the laws and oversees the government (e.g., The President of the United States is a member of the executive branch.)

5. **House of Representatives** — the larger part of Congress; representatives are elected from each state, depending upon the number of people living in that state, for a period of two years

6. **judicial system** — having to do with the courts of law and justice

7. **monarchy** — a type of government where one person, such as a king or queen, rules over the people

8. **Senate** — the smaller part of Congress; two representatives are elected from each state for a period of six years

9. **session** — the period of time each year when Congress is working

10. **veto** — the power that the United States President or a state governor has to keep a bill passed by legislature from becoming a law

② Fill-in-the-Blank — Government

Fill in the blanks with the words or phrases from the box.

Congress	judicial system	veto	democracy	session
executive branch	consent	House of Representatives	Senate	monarchy

1. The power that the President of the United States has to keep a bill from becoming a law is a _____.

2. When Congress is working, they are in _____.

3. The courts of law make up the _____.

4. The President of the United States and the part of the government that carries out the laws and oversees the government is the _____.

5. A government in which people make decisions by voting is a _____.

6. The Senate and the House of Representatives make up _____.

7. The _____ is made of two representatives from each state.

8. A type of government having a king is a _____.

9. When someone gives her _____, she agrees or gives her permission.

10. The larger of the two houses in Congress is the _____.

2 Word Association — Government

Write the word or phrase from the box next to the word or phrase that shares a similar meaning.

| Congress | judicial system | veto | democracy | session |
| executive branch | consent | House of Representatives | Senate | monarchy |

1. stop from becoming law _____

2. Senate and House of Representatives _____

3. government with voters _____

4. larger part of Congress _____

5. time Congress is working _____

6. courts of law _____

7. two from each state _____

8. ruled by king or queen _____

9. President _____

10. permission _____

② Writing Sentences — Government

Write a sentence using each word or phrase.

1. Congress

2. consent

3. democracy

4. executive branch

5. House of Representatives

6. judicial system

7. monarch

8. Senate

9. session

10. veto

Crossword Puzzle — Government

Complete the puzzle with words that match the clues.

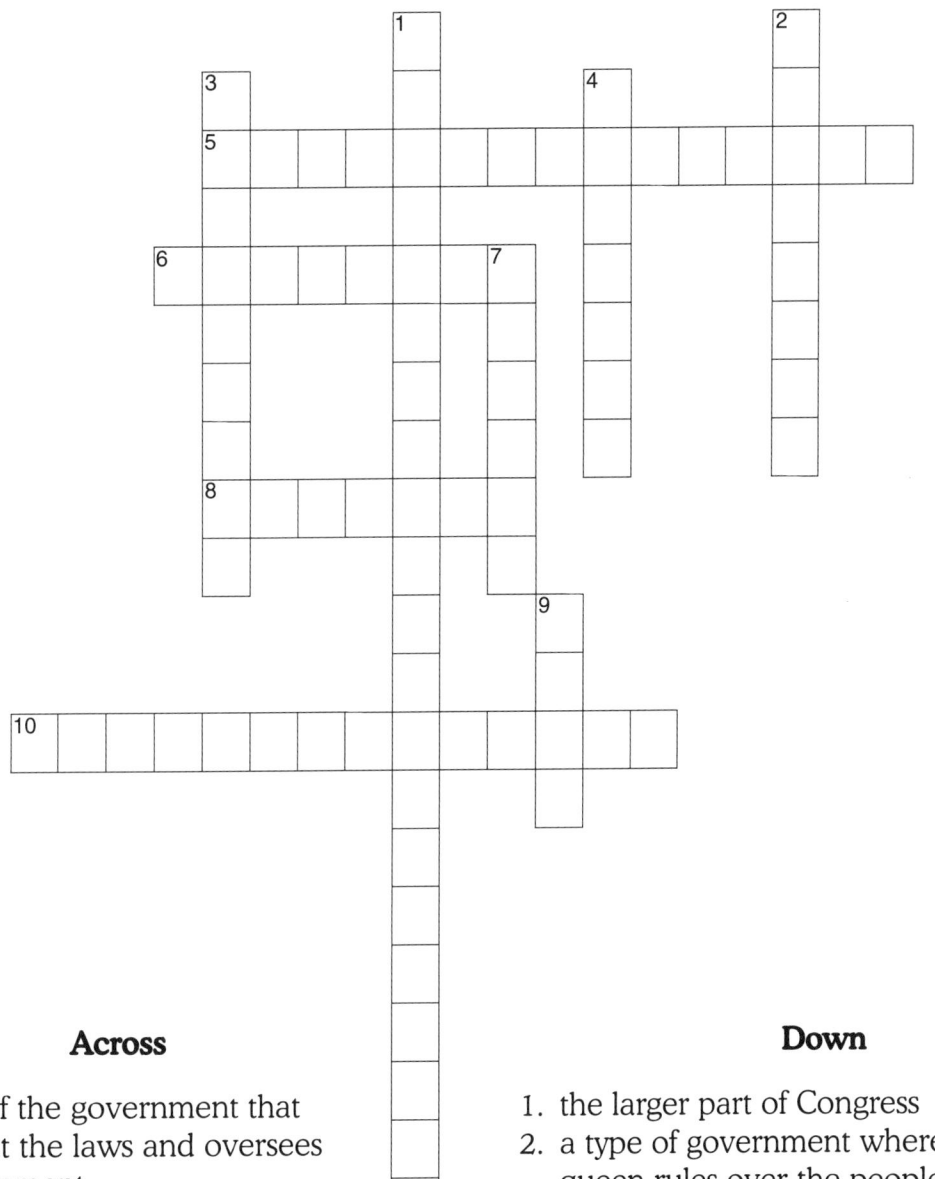

Across

5. the part of the government that carries out the laws and oversees the government
6. the Senate and the House of Representatives
8. to give permission; agree to
10. having to do with courts of law and justice

Down

1. the larger part of Congress
2. a type of government where a king or queen rules over the people
3. a form of government in which people make political decisions by voting
4. the period of time each year when Congress is working
7. the smaller part of Congress; two representatives are elected from each state for a period of six years
9. the power to keep a bill passed by legislature from becoming a law

100% Curriculum Vocabulary—Grades 6-12

② Word Search — Government

All the words or phrases listed in the box appear in the puzzle — horizontally, vertically, diagonally, or backward. Find and circle them.

Congress	judicial system	veto	democracy	session
executive branch	consent	House of Representatives	Senate	monarchy

```
B P V C F A O L W E P T R U D M Y A N F H J
L R I J J N O W U S O H M B N K F Y M Y D G
I N S Z Z I D O D J Q E C H U H I E E N E T
Y M V F P V A E E Y Q Y L Q E S I Y T Q Q G
E B R M P H K U T J T Y U Q Z N C N S I O F
Q X I K Q J C U V E I H J O O A X B Y K Q B
S E V I T A T N E S E R P E R F O E S U O H
M T A X I I B O A G C W W C P D F L L F M E
Y T Z L D L M N I R W M O B J A F L A X P A
P X I B E J R D O S B M K W Z I M A I J N Y
T B F V P M E R H T E E Z L B S C H C A L J
H S M C P N F O M D E J V O I G C J I Y I K
I W L Q T L M I T Y M V C I C V D K D K M S
V M W F N S D S P G P F K O T Y P L U J P E
J G Z T F C I G J P P A N A N U B A J L T S
E T A N E S E G H X Y S G M F G C S G Z I S
T G V T U J H G A V E L A A B B R E P P X I
H S S G J O F V T N G L A J W A B E X M A O
O M J B Q T Z A T N F U L A M V X C S E C N
S L F Z Q I A M Q D J K H A K N M D E S B M
M O N A R C H Y M F S H Y O U D M X L N P A
N Z I R I S B G U Y T G W W R N E S Z D W B
```

100% Curriculum Vocabulary—Grades 6-12

3 Definitions — Government

1. **acquit** — to declare in court that a person is not guilty of a crime

2. **candidate** — a person who seeks or is recommended for some office

3. **debate** — a discussion between people with different opinions

4. **immigrant** — a person who comes into a foreign country to make a new home

5. **indict** — to formally charge someone with a crime by a grand jury

6. **jury** — a group of people who are chosen to listen to the facts and evidence in a law trial and to decide on a verdict (guilty or innocent)

7. **majority** — a number more than half the total

8. **minority** — a number less than half the total

9. **native** — a person who lives in the country in which he or she was born

10. **voter** — a person who makes a choice or decision in an election by voting

3 Fill-in-the-Blank — Government

Fill in the blanks with the words or phrases from the box.

| acquit | debate | indict | majority | native |
| candidate | immigrant | jury | minority | voter |

1. To declare in court that a person is not guilty of a crime is to _____.

2. An _____ is a person who comes into a foreign country to make a new home.

3. A _____ is a number more than half the total.

4. A _____ is a number less than half the total.

5. To _____ someone is to formally charge them with a crime.

6. A _____ is a discussion between people with different opinions.

7. A person who seeks or is recommended for an office is a _____.

8. A person who makes a choice or decision in an election is a _____.

9. A _____ is a group of people who are chosen to listen to the facts and evidence in a law trial and to decide on a verdict.

10. A _____ is a person who lives in the country in which he was born.

3 Word Association — Government

Write the word from the box next to the word or phrase that shares a similar meaning.

| jury | voter | indict | candidate | native |
| majority | minority | acquit | immigrant | debate |

1. group of people who decide a verdict _____
2. decision maker _____
3. person from a foreign country _____
4. lives in country where born _____
5. less than half _____
6. discussion _____
7. to find not guilty _____
8. more than half _____
9. formally charge _____
10. person seeking office _____

3 Writing Sentences — Government

Write a sentence using each word.

1. acquit

2. candidate

3. debate

4. immigrant

5. indict

6. jury

7. majority

8. minority

9. native

10. voter

Crossword Puzzle — Government

Complete the puzzle with words that match the clues.

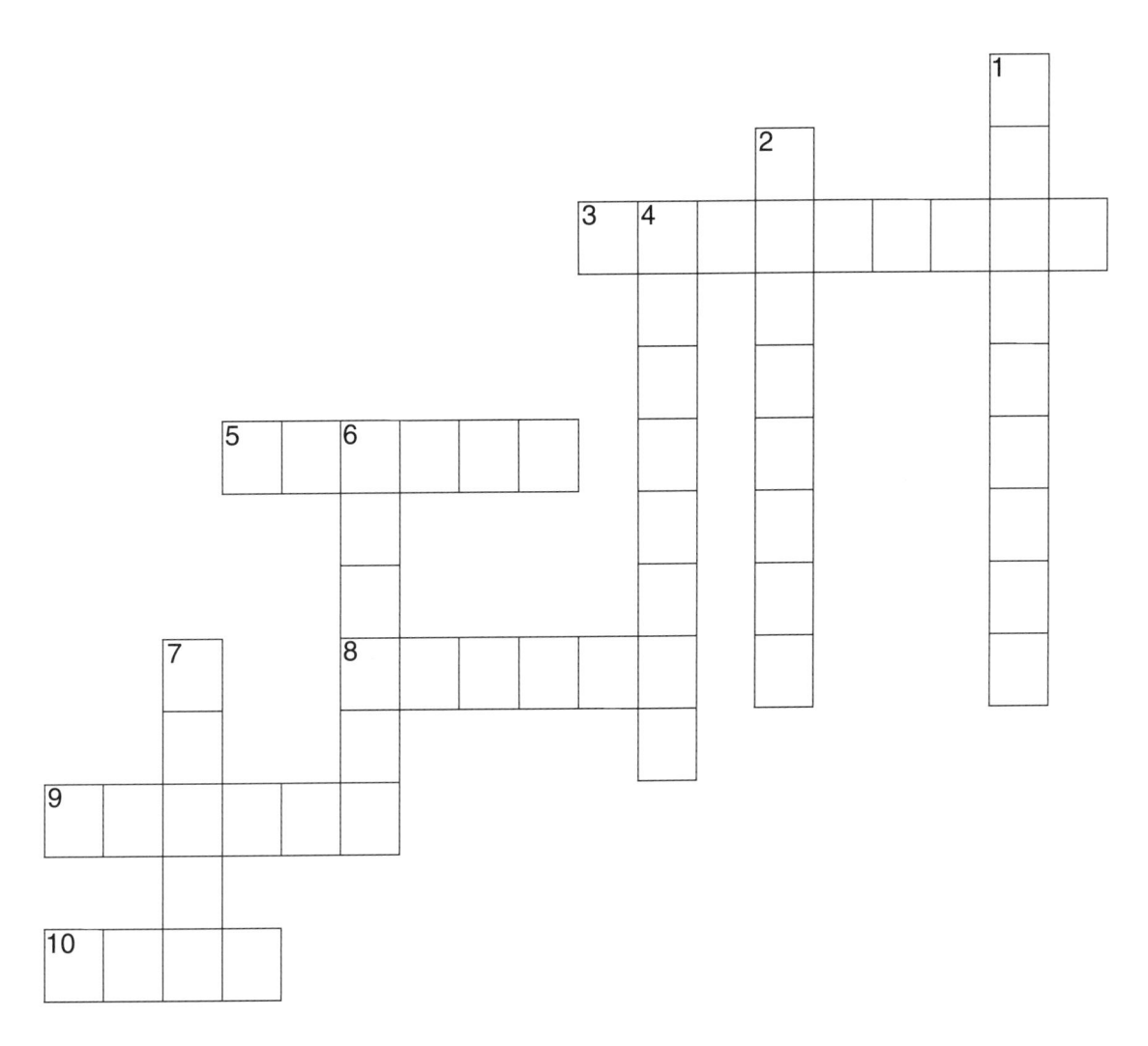

Across

3. a person who comes into a foreign country to make a new home
5. to formally charge someone with a crime
8. to declare in court that a person is not guilty of a crime
9. a person who lives in the country in which he was born
10. a group of people who are chosen to listen to the facts and evidence in a law trial

Down

1. a person who seeks or is recommended for some office
2. a number less than half the total
4. a number more than half the total
6. a discussion between people with different opinions
7. a person who makes a choice or decision in an election by voting

3 Word Search — Government

All the words or phrases listed in the box appear in the puzzle — horizontally, vertically, diagonally, or backward. Find and circle them.

acquit	debate	indict	majority	native
candidate	immigrant	jury	minority	voter

```
E F G F P T M C C R U A Z S Y
Q T C V I T V A T K A R L T T
B M N D I A N I N D I C T P I
D U Y U B D K U B S M P T R R
W E Q X I T N A R G I M M I O
Y C B D L X A R I Z C V U D N
A T A A I G T J G X D G E L I
N T I C T P I L F N H R Q U M
E Z J R L E V X G C Y U T H W
A O U O O V E G B Y I N U M X
J O C J O J M E Z D G T S L Y
C O S T A N A Y R U J Q O L P
S U E Q Q A T M J V L W E H W
N R Q P V D L M M L D V O D N
T Z P D D J C B J X A W F O O
```

100% Curriculum Vocabulary—Grades 6-12

① Definitions — Health

1. **abuse** — physical, emotional, or mental mistreatment of another person

2. **body language** — communication or messages given through body movements, facial expressions, and gestures rather than through words

3. **denial** — refusing to recognize an emotion or problem or to accept reality

4. **displacement** — having bad feelings toward someone not really related to the cause of a problem

5. **emotion** — a strong feeling, such as love, anger, or fear

6. **extrovert** — a friendly person who likes being around people

7. **introvert** — a reserved person who is quiet and shy

8. **neglect** — not providing the basic physical and emotional needs to a person, such as food, clothing, housing, love, and encouragement

9. **personality** — qualities and characteristics, such as behaviors, thoughts, or feelings that make each person different from everyone else

10. **risk behavior** — behavior that increases your chance of being harmed or harming others

1 Fill-in-the-Blank — Health

Fill in the blanks with the words or phrases from the box.

| displacement | body language | abuse | denial | risk behavior |
| neglect | introvert | emotion | personality | extrovert |

1. _____ occurs when you have bad feelings towards someone who is not related to the cause of a problem.

2. A friendly, outgoing person is an _____.

3. A person's _____ is the behaviors, thoughts, or feelings that make each person different.

4. A quiet, shy person who is reserved is an _____.

5. Communication through body movements instead of words is _____.

6. _____ is physical, emotional, or mental mistreatment of another person.

7. _____ is refusing to recognize a problem or to accept reality.

8. An _____ is a strong feeling, such as love, anger, or fear.

9. Not providing someone with food, clothing, and love are forms of _____.

10. Behavior that increases your chance of being harmed or harming others is a _____.

1 Word Association — Health

Write the word or phrase from the box next to the word or phrase that shares a similar meaning.

> displacement   body language   abuse   denial   risk behavior
> neglect   introvert   emotion   personality   extrovert

1. a feeling _____

2. blame innocent person _____

3. body movements _____

4. outgoing person _____

5. not providing basic needs _____

6. behavior that causes harm _____

7. shy person _____

8. mistreatment of others _____

9. ignoring a problem _____

10. a person's characteristics _____

① Writing Sentences — Health

Write a sentence using each word or phrase.

1. abuse

2. body language

3. denial

4. displacement

5. emotion

6. extrovert

7. introvert

8. neglect

9. personality

10. risk behavior

Crossword Puzzle — Health

Complete the puzzle with words that match the clues.

Across

1. not providing the basic physical and emotional needs to a person
6. a reserved person who is quiet and shy
7. mistreatment of another person
8. characteristics that make each person different from everyone else
9. a friendly person who likes being around people
10. communication through body movements or facial expressions rather than words

Down

2. a strong feeling, such as love, anger, or fear
3. behavior that increases your chances of being harmed
4. having bad feelings toward someone not really related to the cause of a problem
5. refusing to recognize an emotion or problem or to accept reality

1 Word Search — Health

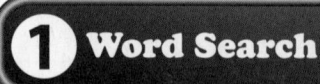

All the words or phrases listed in the box appear in the puzzle — horizontally, vertically, diagonally, or backward. Find and circle them.

- displacement
- body language
- abuse
- denial
- risk behavior
- neglect
- introvert
- emotion
- personality
- extrovert

```
P H F T U S D V M A Y E R B D
N E G L E C T V F Y G Q I T E
V N B J P M T X K A F A S T N
G J J L I Y H X U P B K K R I
F L G U J L B G H U I H B E A
Q Y T I L A N O S R E P E V L
D I S P L A C E M E N T H O Q
J E F Z L K B M F R R H A R Q
R G M Y H Y A M B E O X V T A
Z F D O R L U X V K C R I N F
C O K O T F J O I Y O Y O I B
B R V X X I R C C X O J R U Q
O H P O X T O C A B D M X O L
F C F D X O T N J L I N Z H A
C O Q E A G V W M R L O A L C
```

100% Curriculum Vocabulary—Grades 6-12   Copyright © 2002 LinguiSystems, Inc.

② Definitions — Health

1. **emphysema** — a lung disease that causes extreme breathing difficulties

2. **high blood pressure** — excessive pressure against the walls of blood vessels, also known as *hypertension*

3. **homeostasis** — the state of the body when it functions normally and is balanced

4. **quality of life** — how satisfying and meaningful a person's life is

5. **sleep apnea** — an illness that causes a person to stop breathing many times during a night's sleep

6. **stress** — pressure or strain on the mind and body due to the body's response to change

7. **stroke** — a serious condition that occurs when the blood supply to the brain is cut off, usually due to a blockage in the artery that goes to the brain

8. **ulcer** — an open sore on the inner wall of the stomach or small intestine

9. **values** — beliefs or ideals that guide your actions and help you know what is right or wrong

10. **wellness** — an overall condition of total physical, mental, and social health

2 Fill-in-the-Blank — Health

Fill in the blanks with the words or phrases from the box.

| emphysema | homeostasis | high blood pressure | values | wellness |
| ulcer | sleep apnea | stress | stroke | quality of life |

1. An open sore on the wall of the stomach or small intestine is an _____.

2. Your _____ is how satisfying and meaningful your life is.

3. People who suffer from _____ have extreme difficulty breathing.

4. _____ is pressure or strain on the mind and body.

5. Someone who has a blockage in an artery that goes to the brain may experience a serious condition called a _____.

6. _____, or hypertension, is excessive pressure on the walls of blood vessels.

7. An overall condition of total health is _____.

8. If the body functions normally and is balanced, it's in a state of _____.

9. _____ causes a person to stop breathing many times during the night.

10. _____ are beliefs or ideals that guide your actions and help you know what is right or wrong.

② Word Association — Health

Write the word or phrase from the box next to the word or phrase that shares a similar meaning.

emphysema	homeostasis	high blood pressure	values	wellness
ulcer	sleep apnea	stress	stroke	quality of life

1. open sore _____

2. satisfying and meaningful life _____

3. normal functioning _____

4. stop breathing at night _____

5. pressure or strain on the mind _____

6. beliefs or ideals _____

7. total overall health _____

8. blood supply to brain cut off _____

9. hypertension _____

10. difficulty breathing _____

② Writing Sentences — Health

Write a sentence using each word or phrase.

1. emphysema

2. high blood pressure

3. homeostasis

4. quality of life

5. sleep apnea

6. stress

7. stroke

8. ulcer

9. values

10. wellness

Crossword Puzzle — Health

Complete the puzzle with words that match the clues.

Across

4. how satisfying and meaningful a person's life is
5. the state of the body when it functions normally and is balanced
7. an illness which causes a person to stop breathing many times during each night
9. an overall condition of total health
10. pressure or strain on the mind and body

Down

1. beliefs or ideals that guide your actions and help you know what is right or wrong
2. a serious condition that occurs when the blood supply to the brain is cut off
3. extreme pressure against the walls of blood vessels
6. a lung disease that causes breathing difficulties
8. an open sore in the stomach or small intestine

100% Curriculum Vocabulary—Grades 6-12

② Word Search — Health

All the words or phrases listed in the box appear in the puzzle — horizontally, vertically, diagonally, or backward. Find and circle them.

emphysema	homeostasis	high blood pressure	values	wellness
ulcer	sleep apnea	stress	stroke	quality of life

```
W S H P M A X W M W A U A T B K H
U Z I B T C D M C M H D A V G I B
G P D S E U Q F E O Y N W X G A E
Z Y N I A D H S M N Q T H H U E S
Z Q W S P T Y B F X D U B I W N T
U C W K T H S H H X H L V P X P B
K L V F P R Q O X B O S V H S A I
W R F M K N E D E O S A N L T P Y
B R E C L U R S D M L V I E R E K
L J Z T M G J P S U O K F M O E Z
E K P T T J R U E O B H H W K L D
W E L L N E S S L I M H D C E S B
C G E S S T S A W Q K W O A B U L
O X A S J L H D O R L P N U M K M
Z W U E F I L F O Y T I L A U Q U
Z R J Z Q N R O Z M Z F H A I R S
E T O X P O Y O H N A T Y J M V P
```

100% Curriculum Vocabulary—Grades 6-12

3 Definitions — Health

1. **adrenaline** — a hormone that increases breathing, heart rate, and the level of sugar in the blood thereby giving the body extra energy to respond to emergencies

2. **carbohydrates** — nutrients, such as sugar and starches, that are the main sources of energy to the body

3. **carcinogen** — something that causes cancer, such as cigarette smoke

4. **dehydration** — the drying out of the body, body tissues, and/or body fluids

5. **digestion** — the process of changing foods (breaking them down) into a form that the body can use

6. **habit** — something a person does so often or so long that it is done without thinking; usually hard to stop or control

7. **immune system** — the body's natural, built-in defense system that fights germs that enter the body

8. **metabolism** — the rate at which the body changes nutrients into energy and tissue

9. **narcotic** — an addictive drug used to relieve pain and help you sleep; can only be legally obtained with a doctor's prescription

10. **physical environment** — all of the elements that surround you, such as air and water; you depend on it to live

3 Fill-in-the-Blank — Health

Fill in the blanks with the words or phrases from the box.

| adrenaline | carcinogen | digestion | dehydration | metabolism |
| carbohydrates | habit | physical environment | immune system | narcotic |

1. The _____ is the body's natural, built-in defense system that fights germs that enter the body.

2. Your _____ is all of the elements that surround you.

3. An example of a _____ is cigarette smoke.

4. _____ are nutrients, like sugar and starches, that are the main sources of energy to the body.

5. _____ is the process of breaking down foods into a form that the body can use.

6. An addictive drug used to relieve pain is a _____.

7. _____ occurs when body tissues and body fluids are dry.

8. A person's _____ is the rate at which the person's body changes nutrients into energy and tissue.

9. A _____ is something a person does so often or so long that it is done without thinking.

10. _____ is a hormone that increases breathing, heart rate, and the level of sugar in the blood thereby giving the body extra energy to respond to emergencies.

3 Word Association — Health

Write the word or phrase from the box next to the word or phrase that shares a similar meaning.

| adrenaline | carcinogen | digestion | dehydration | metabolism |
| carbohydrates | habit | physical environment | immune system | narcotic |

1. biting your fingernails _____

2. elements around you _____

3. cigarette smoke _____

4. sugar and starches _____

5. changes nutrients into energy _____

6. body's natural defense _____

7. hormone that gives extra energy _____

8. breaking down food _____

9. addictive drug _____

10. body drying out _____

3 Writing Sentences — Health

Write a sentence using each word or phrase.

1. adrenaline _____
   _____

2. carbohydrates _____
   _____

3. carcinogen _____
   _____

4. dehydration _____
   _____

5. digestion _____
   _____

6. habit _____
   _____

7. immune system _____
   _____

8. metabolism _____
   _____

9. narcotic _____
   _____

10. physical environment _____
    _____

100% Curriculum Vocabulary—Grades 6-12   Copyright © 2002 LinguiSystems, Inc.

③ Crossword Puzzle — Health

Complete the puzzle with words that match the clues.

Across

3. something that causes cancer
5. the breaking down of food into a form that the body can use
6. nutrients, such as sugar and starches, that are the main source of energy to the body
9. an addictive drug used to relieve pain
10. the body's natural, built-in defense system

Down

1. all of the elements that surround you
2. the rate at which the body changes nutrients into energy and tissue
4. a hormone that increases breathing, heart rate, and the level of sugar in the blood
7. something a person does so often that it is done without thinking
8. the drying out of the body, body tissues, and/or body fluids

100% Curriculum Vocabulary—Grades 6-12

③ Word Search — Health

All the words or phrases listed in the box appear in the puzzle — horizontally, vertically, diagonally, or backward. Find and circle them.

adrenaline	carcinogen	digestion	dehydration	metabolism
carbohydrates	habit	physical environment	immune system	narcotic

```
Y D Z Z M G W H H W J L X E L Q L K E
F I B K Z S B E N A R D U N K Z D A H
H T W B M C I X M J B N A R C O T I C
P H Y S I C A L E N V I R O N M E N T
M I Y Y M V E R O D J S T F B S T I M
R N O B M V Y X B B V L T W D X L W C
Z E E O U N I J T O A B Y E E K W H G
I G B Z N J Q Q I N H T H T K S I T Q
P O E R E M N L G N Z Y E J C Z E B G
B N O I S O D P O T D Z D M V R F W U
H I H D Y T J I G R U E Y R C V V B T
A C U V S W T L A N Z M S P A I D A C
T R G Y T S V T H Q V H R J H T I W W
R A O D E N I L A N E R D A F B E H O
H C G G M O X L T Q O I Y W P D U S V
T Y I Z N V J P R A F Z C F G F S T V
G D I Q C W S E O L J N B N K R X I B
R F P Z D P P B V X O N S S D C C H J
Q D P Q T M X A X G C Z R I A A G Q D
```

100% Curriculum Vocabulary—Grades 6-12

4 Definitions — Health

1. **asthma** — a disease that causes a person to have trouble breathing; often includes bouts of coughing

2. **astigmatism** — an eye condition caused by an uneven curving of the lens of the eye, resulting in blurred vision

3. **color blindness** — a condition of not being able to see the difference between certain colors

4. **diaphragm** — a muscle that separates the chest from the stomach

5. **epilepsy** — a disorder of the nervous system causing people to have seizures

6. **Eustachian tube** — a tube running from the inner ear to the back of the throat that helps equalize the air pressure on both sides of the eardrum

7. **Fetal Alcohol Syndrome** — physical and mental problems that can occur in the child of a woman who drinks too much alcohol during pregnancy

8. **gingivitis** — a common gum disease caused by bacteria between the teeth in which gums become red and swollen and bleed easily

9. **plaque** — a colorless, thin film of bacteria that forms on teeth

10. **vaccination** — a shot to protect a person from getting a disease

4 Fill-in-the-Blank — Health

Fill in the blanks with the words or phrases from the box.

| asthma | Eustachian tube | Fetal Alcohol Syndrome | vaccination | diaphragm |
| epilepsy | astigmatism | plaque | color blindness | gingivitis |

1. A _____ is a shot that protects a person from getting a disease.

2. An _____ is an eye condition in which vision is blurred.

3. The _____ is a muscle that helps breathing.

4. The tube that runs from the inner ear to the back of the throat is the _____.

5. People brush their teeth to remove the _____, or the thin film of bacteria that forms on teeth.

6. _____ is a disorder of the nervous system causing people to have seizures.

7. Drinking while pregnant can cause _____.

8. A disease in which gums become swollen and bleed easily is _____.

9. A person who has difficulty breathing may have _____.

10. _____ is a condition of not being able to see the difference between certain colors.

④ Word Association — Health

Write the word or phrase from the box next to the word or phrase that shares a similar meaning.

| asthma | Eustachian tube | Fetal Alcohol Syndrome | vaccination | diaphragm |
| epilepsy | astigmatism | plaque | color blindness | gingivitis |

1. part of the ear _____

2. blurry vision _____

3. breathing disease _____

4. seizures _____

5. shot _____

6. drinking during pregnancy causes it _____

7. muscle _____

8. vision condition _____

9. gum disease _____

10. film of bacteria _____

100% Curriculum Vocabulary—Grades 6-12

4 Writing Sentences — Health

Write a sentence using each word or phrase.

1. asthma

2. astigmatism

3. color blindness

4. diaphragm

5. epilepsy

6. Eustachian tube

7. Fetal Alcohol Syndrome

8. gingivitis

9. plaque

10. vaccination

Crossword Puzzle — Health

Complete the puzzle with words that match the clues.

Across

2. a disease that causes a person to have trouble breathing
3. a colorless, thin film of bacteria that forms on teeth
6. a shot that protects a person from getting a disease
8. an eye condition in which vision is blurred
9. a gum disease in which gums become red and swollen and bleed easily
10. physical and mental problems that occur in the child of a woman who drinks too much alcohol during pregnancy

Down

1. a muscle that separates the chest from the stomach
4. a disorder of the nervous system causing people to have seizures
5. a tube running from the inner ear to the back of the throat that helps equalize the air pressure
7. a condition of not being able to see the difference between certain colors

④ Word Search — Health

All the words or phrases listed in the box appear in the puzzle — horizontally, vertically, diagonally, or backward. Find and circle them.

asthma	Eustachian tube	Fetal Alcohol Syndrome	vaccination	diaphragm
epilepsy	astigmatism	plaque	color blindness	gingivitis

```
S G O O W O I G E Y A U I N A V N O B B F
S R I L O A S P X B N F Y G Y E V J G K U T
E I N N T G I D Q F U V Y W N W V H M T C V
N Z J K G L T Z E S E T A I T X M F R N L C
D A S R E I E P U A O F N Q U A C P L L T B
N X X P I V V M V T A P N A P D P T T L M T
I T S M N N B I X N D T O R I E U Q A L P N
L Y J W Q I C I T Q I D J F Q H J M T O E M
B R N S B N E D T I A K D V E Z C A U G J H
R U D F P Q I M F T S M I A A L F A I S S P
O X F W N O I P M G M M A T Y E M K T K W Z
L M A Y M A H M B A F C P B P S G C B S V V
O Q T Z E S P P G A I B H S I A N G X K U O
C V A C C I N A T I O N R T I D W R T A W E
A F M K T G A E S V B V A R G A E S P E N M
C I I L G A Q Q F X Q M G L P G M D H F J H
R Z R U D U W R O Q G G M Z P C M H W M Y I
Z C I Y C B S E T I M L D N O O G E T P M J
L L M Z Q T B D T Y X N B O C B M L J S Y Z
E M O R D N Y S L O H O C L A L A T E F A X
J X N A X Y A O Q E F Z C V E O E P F P W C
D X A S H T T Y R M G Y L X X G P K U V X Z
```

100% Curriculum Vocabulary—Grades 6-12

5 Definitions — Health

1. **amnesia** — a sudden loss of memory

2. **anorexia nervosa** — an eating disorder in which a person refuses to eat or is always dieting to lose weight due to an intense fear of weight gain

3. **anxiety disorder** — a disorder in which real or imagined fears and excessive worrying keep a person from enjoying a normal life

4. **bulimia** — an eating disorder in which a person eats large amounts of food and then tries to get rid of the food by vomiting

5. **depression** — feelings of hopelessness, inability to eat or sleep, and a loss of interest in life

6. **manic-depressive disorder** — extreme mood swings from happy to depressed for no reason; also known as *bi-polar disorder*

7. **obsessive-compulsive disorder** — the need to do things in a certain way over and over again combined with the inability to stop

8. **phobia** — a strong, unexplainable fear of an object, situation, or person that is so great that it interferes with reasonable action

9. **psychiatrist** — a doctor who is specially trained to treat people who have serious mental problems

10. **schizophrenia** — a serious mental disorder in which a person's thoughts disagree with reality, such as hearing imaginary voices

5 Fill-in-the-Blank — Health

Fill in the blanks with the words or phrases from the box.

```
psychiatrist    manic-depressive disorder    anorexia nervosa    obsessive-compulsive disorder    schizophrenia

amnesia    anxiety disorder    depression    bulimia    phobia
```

1. _____ is a serious mental disorder in which a person's thoughts disagree with reality.

2. A person who suffers a sudden loss of memory may have _____.

3. A _____ is a fear that is so great that it interferes with reasonable action.

4. A person with _____ refuses to eat or is always dieting to lose weight.

5. A doctor who treats people who are mentally ill is a _____.

6. _____ is the need to do things in a certain way over and over again, combined with the inability to stop.

7. _____ involves hopelessness and a loss of interest in life.

8. _____, or bi-polar disorder, causes extreme mood swings from happy to depressed for no reason.

9. Eating large amounts of food and then vomiting is a sign of _____.

10. An _____ causes a person to have real or imagined fears and worries that keep the person from enjoying a normal life.

5 Word Association — Health

Write the word or phrase from the box next to the word or phrase that shares a similar meaning.

psychiatrist	manic-depressive disorder	anorexia nervosa	obsessive-compulsive disorder	schizophrenia
amnesia	anxiety disorder	depression	bulimia	phobia

1. memory loss _____

2. over and over _____

3. extreme mood swings _____

4. vomiting _____

5. unexplainable fear _____

6. disorder of real or imagined fears _____

7. treats people with mental problems _____

8. not eating _____

9. feelings of hopelessness _____

10. thoughts disagree with reality _____

100% Curriculum Vocabulary—Grades 6-12

5 Writing Sentences — Health

Write a sentence using each word or phrase.

1. amnesia

2. anorexia nervosa

3. anxiety disorder

4. bulimia

5. depression

6. manic-depressive disorder

7. obsessive-compulsive disorder

8. phobia

9. psychiatrist

10. schizophrenia

100% Curriculum Vocabulary—Grades 6-12

Crossword Puzzle — Health

Complete the puzzle with words that match the clues.

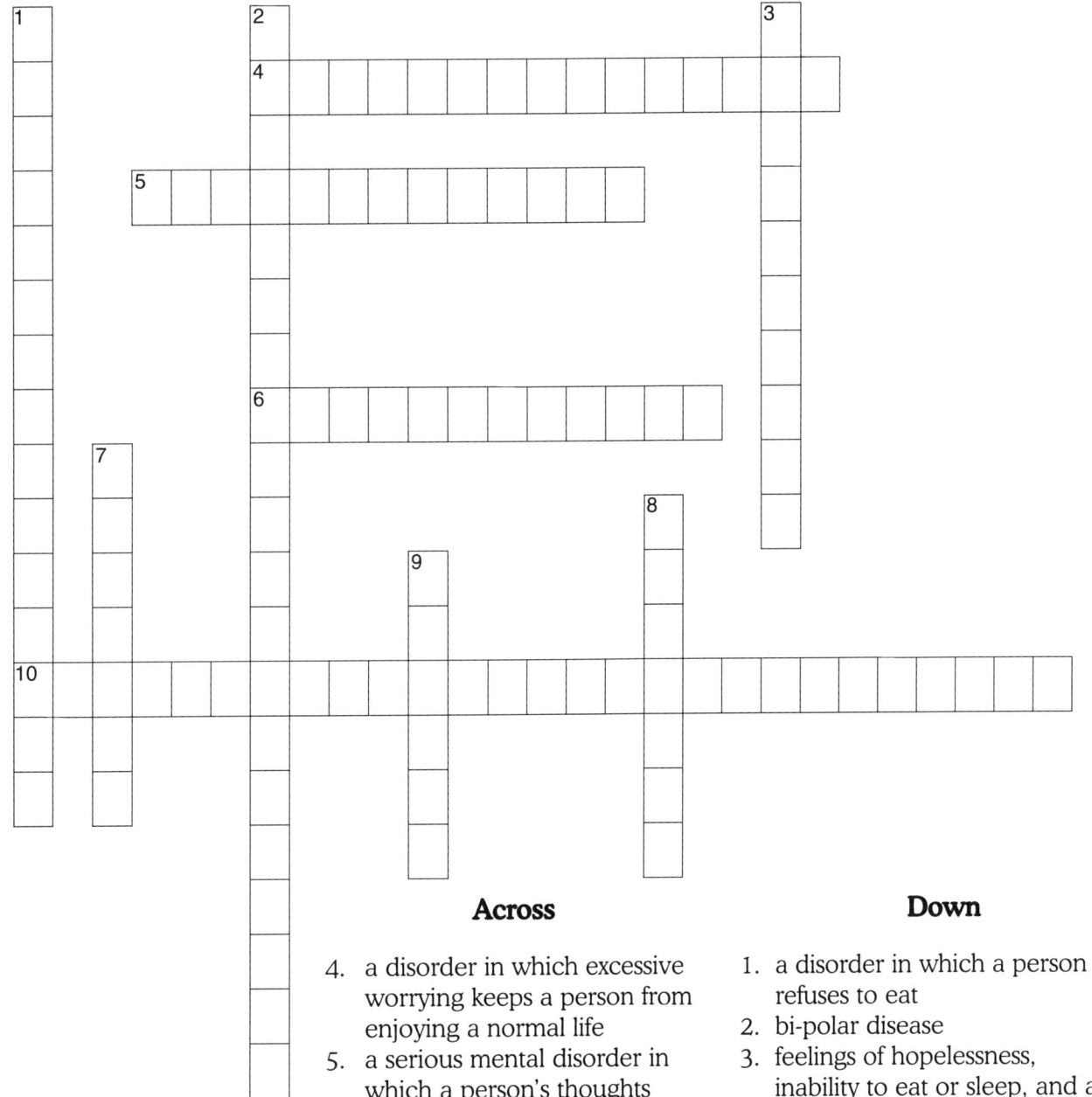

Across

4. a disorder in which excessive worrying keeps a person from enjoying a normal life
5. a serious mental disorder in which a person's thoughts disagree with reality
6. a doctor who treats people who have serious mental problems
10. the need to do things in a certain way over and over again with the inability to stop

Down

1. a disorder in which a person refuses to eat
2. bi-polar disease
3. feelings of hopelessness, inability to eat or sleep, and a loss of interest in life
7. a sudden loss of memory
8. a disorder in which a person eats large amounts of food and then vomits
9. a strong, unexplainable fear of an object, situation, or person

100% Curriculum Vocabulary—Grades 6-12

⑤ Word Search — Health

All the words or phrases listed in the box appear in the puzzle — horizontally, vertically, diagonally, or backward. Find and circle them.

psychiatrist	manic-depressive disorder	anorexia nervosa	obsessive-compulsive disorder	schizophrenia
amnesia	anxiety disorder	depression	bulimia	phobia

```
L S Y M E V W V X M H L W P A Q D M G D Y L N E M B E X
R P C V Q K M K U V V M E S I Z U Y A U N F B P Q P X B
J E L H Q S J X H T K N O Y B F V U R C K N K P D Z N B
M W D Y I N Y J I B V V M C O R D F Q S Q D S A P A A P
R N T R X Z M E S Q R P Z H H B J I M P U E X A W D R N
Q S T O O H O Z W E Y I K I P Z Q H R W A H N E R X E B
N F P E V S Q P N U Q Q Q A P A D J W B Z M C D P C D Z
J T P Y I H I A H Z F R C T I A R P N L O Q R K V V R J
Z H X A N O I D B R A J N R P M E U B E L H S Y C U O C
H U U C O X G S E P E G X I V I I F Z Z Z G U V T C S E
M U F G E Z F L O V K N D S I F Z L F A K N E M I H I S
P Y T R S Y M L L U I Q I T N Q E O U M W N V C W G D M
R R O F S W Q E U I T S X A U Y F O Y B K I A C M P E U
I N I W Z Y F D N R H F L R F Y X Y S V H X Y A O K V I
A L Y V Z F Q T M D A Q V U G L A U H U W R L E M C I W
Y D F F C R C J O R H S E F P U G P V E J Q W Z N D S Q
R I K K M W F C I U G P F K V M X P Q E Z C Z Y E V S L
O Q P Q Q P G L G X E D Y X K I O B N Q I C K P Z M E K
U P W V U S J G F X T O D Q D Q E C A W B P R W D G R F
U N Y W X F U S O X E N G M N H Z P E N W E V R V H P M
A B A M P R L N D S T Q T C C J P T U V S M T R Y M E O
H J V X C M A C R U J Q Q J J P E U F S I Y Q C O J D J
F M B Z K W C Q I T U S W G K S N M I D K S D X H D C P
R S R W R P U L G H T V R P K K O O F Z O Q S L Y Y I X
B F Y P R J W B A L P G T U E V N J F I L L H E H H N C
D V U O E A N X I E T Y D I S O R D E R Q Q H K S Y A B
D Q F K R H K U A F E R C S C D O Z H M S E D E I B M S
A I S E N M A S F G U A T J T R M L W H S S M R L G O Z
```

100% Curriculum Vocabulary—Grades 6-12

Definitions — History

1. **abolitionist** — a person who wanted to end slavery in the United States in the years before the Civil War

2. **blockade** — the blocking of a place by an army or navy to stop supplies or people from going in or out

3. **carpetbaggers** — Northerners who went south after the Civil War and tried to gain political power

4. **Confederacy** — the 11 Southern states that separated from the northern United States during the Civil War

5. **indentured servants** — people who agreed to work without pay for a specific period of time in exchange for a boat ticket from Europe to the colonies

6. **plantation** — a large farm, usually in the southern states, on which farm workers live and raise crops such as tobacco, sugar, cotton, and coffee

7. **secede** — to withdraw or separate from a country or a group

8. **sharecropping** — farming on land owned by another person and giving part of the harvest to the landowner as payment or rent

9. **Underground Railroad** — a secret route that helped slaves escape to freedom in the North

10. **Union** — the northern states that were against slavery and remained united under the Constitution during the Civil War

1 Fill-in-the-Blank — History

Fill in the blanks with the words or phrases from the box.

abolitionist	Underground Railroad	indentured servants	sharecropping	plantation
Confederacy	blockade	secede	carpetbaggers	Union

1. _____ agreed to work without pay in exchange for a boat ticket from Europe to the colonies.

2. A _____ is a large farm, usually in the southern states, on which farm workers live and raise crops, such as tobacco, sugar, cotton, and coffee.

3. The northern states who were against slavery were called the _____.

4. The _____ was a secret route that helped slaves escape to freedom in the North.

5. A person who worked to end slavery was an _____.

6. To withdraw or separate from a country or group is to _____.

7. The 11 southern states during the Civil War were the _____.

8. _____ were Northerners who went south after the Civil War and tried to gain political power.

9. A _____ is the blocking of a place to stop supplies from going in or out.

10. _____ is farming on land owned by another person and giving part of the harvest to the landowner as payment or rent.

1. Word Association — History

Write the word or phrase from the box next to the word or phrase that shares a similar meaning.

abolitionist	Underground Railroad	indentured servants	sharecropping	plantation
Confederacy	blockade	secede	carpetbaggers	Union

1. work without pay _____

2. blocking of a place _____

3. states against slavery _____

4. person against slavery _____

5. large Southern farm _____

6. farming land owned by others _____

7. escape route for slaves _____

8. withdraw or separate _____

9. 11 Southern states _____

10. Northerners who went South _____

1 Writing Sentences — History

Write a sentence using each word or phrase.

1. abolitionist

2. blockade

3. carpetbaggers

4. Confederacy

5. indentured servants

6. plantation

7. secede

8. sharecropping

9. Underground Railroad

10. Union

Crossword Puzzle — History

Complete the puzzle with words that match the clues.

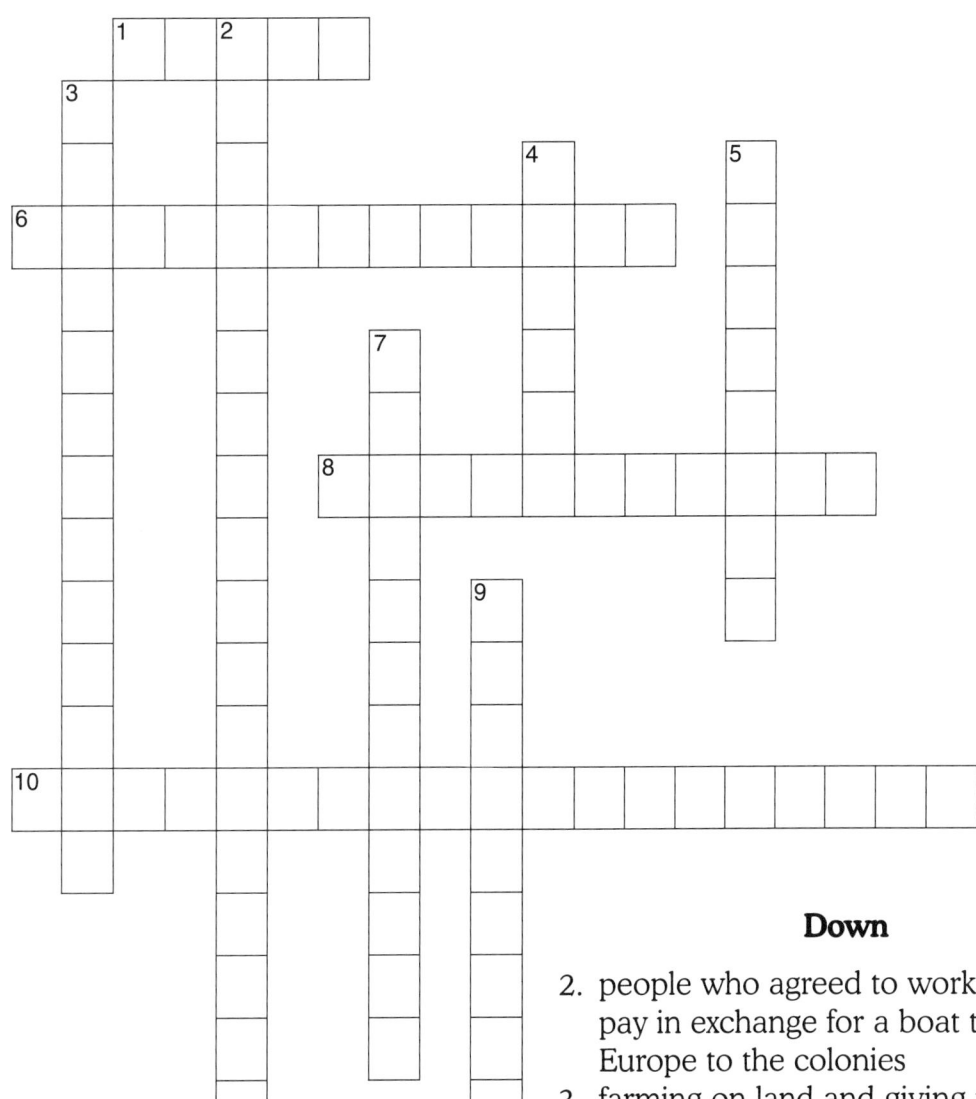

Across

1. the northern states that were against slavery during the Civil War
6. Northerners who went south after the Civil War and tried to gain political power
8. the 11 Southern states that separated from the U.S. during the Civil War
10. a secret route that helped slaves escape to freedom in the North

Down

2. people who agreed to work without pay in exchange for a boat ticket from Europe to the colonies
3. farming on land and giving part of the harvest to the landowner as payment or rent
4. to withdraw or separate from a country or a group
5. the blocking of a place by an army or navy to stop supplies or people from going in or out
7. a person who wanted to end slavery
9. a large farm, usually in southern states, on which farm workers live and raise crops

Word Search — History

All the words or phrases listed in the box appear in the puzzle — horizontally, vertically, diagonally, or backward. Find and circle them.

abolitionist	Underground Railroad	indentured servants	sharecropping	plantation
Confederacy	blockade	secede	carpetbaggers	Union

```
U E G M K J I E X O P Y W H F A A E U
X Z D E N M P K E L W P G D S D P N G
P S Z E V K P A A T S T P B A I D P N
G Z R H C M M N Z E K J M L H E R E I
Y L O E P E T T B Y A Y K F R K N I P
T A X K G A S C L H Q Q K G V C O Z P
A I J S T G A Z R I S P R A W O I L O
J Z N I L Z A M D L P O E O P N N X R
C S O W N I A B F S U D L N G F U K C
H N K N A N O W T N Y H B I A E S B E
S T N A V R E S D E R U T N E D N I R
O N W A W P B R M P P E I X W E Z G A
E J Z X M P A U F V F R O I C R O F H
P C T N H I G Q W F Y K A Z W A B Z S
B A B O L I T I O N I S T C O C J A C
E V E R K L P F N R N X F H V Y W X X
E N O D R R U M T M K O A O B K D J L
C A V I Q E D A K C O L B L J F S E I
D U S H S T U N B A L G Z E J O C C F
```

100% Curriculum Vocabulary—Grades 6-12

② Definitions — History

1. **anti-Semitism** hatred toward or discrimination against people who are Jewish

2. **concentration camp** a prison camp for people who are feared by a government

3. **dictator** a ruler of a country who has complete power

4. **emigrate** to leave one's home country to move to another

5. **Holocaust** the mass killing of European Jews by Nazi Germany during World War II

6. **invasion** entering a country as an enemy to try to take control

7. **overthrow** to replace one government with another using violence

8. **ration** to limit the amount of something given out, such as gas and food, usually during a war

9. **refugees** people who flee from a place to find safety and protection somewhere else

10. **traitor** a person who betrays his own country and helps its enemies

2 Fill-in-the-Blank — History

Fill in the blanks with the words or phrases from the box.

| anti-Semitism | overthrow | concentration camp | ration | invasion |
| emigrate | traitor | Holocaust | dictator | refugees |

1. Entering a country as an enemy to try to take control is an _____.

2. To _____ is to limit the amount of something given out.

3. _____ are people who flee from a place to find safety somewhere else.

4. A person who betrays his own country and helps its enemies is a _____.

5. To _____ is to replace one government with another using violence.

6. Hatred toward or discrimination against people who are Jewish is _____.

7. A _____ is a prison camp for people who are feared by a government.

8. A ruler of a country who has complete power is a _____.

9. To leave your home country to move to another is to _____.

10. The mass killing of European Jews by Nazi Germany was the _____.

② Word Association — History

Write the word or phrase from the box next to the word or phrase that shares a similar meaning.

| anti-Semitism | overthrow | concentration camp | ration | invasion |
| emigrate | traitor | Holocaust | dictator | refugees |

1. person who betrays _____

2. ruler with complete power _____

3. entering a country to take control _____

4. replace a government using violence _____

5. mass killing of European Jews _____

6. prison camp _____

7. leave home country _____

8. limited amount of something _____

9. people looking for safety _____

10. discrimination against Jews _____

2 Writing Sentences — History

Write a sentence using each word or phrase.

1. anti-Semitism _____
   _____

2. concentration camp _____
   _____

3. dictator _____
   _____

4. emigrate _____
   _____

5. Holocaust _____
   _____

6. invasion _____
   _____

7. overthrow _____
   _____

8. ration _____
   _____

9. refugees _____
   _____

10. traitor _____
    _____

100% Curriculum Vocabulary—Grades 6-12

Crossword Puzzle — History

Complete the puzzle with words that match the clues.

Across

3. the mass killing of European Jews by Nazi Germany during World War II
6. hatred toward or discrimination against people who are Jewish
7. a ruler of a country who has complete power
8. to leave one's home country to move to another
9. people who flee from a place to find safety and protection somewhere else
10. to limit the amount of something given out

Down

1. a person who betrays his own country and helps its enemies
2. entering a country as an enemy to try to take control
4. to replace one government with another using violence
5. a prison camp for people who are feared by a government

② Word Search — History

All the words or phrases listed in the box appear in the puzzle — horizontally, vertically, diagonally, or backward. Find and circle them.

anti-Semitism	overthrow	concentration camp	ration	invasion
emigrate	traitor	Holocaust	dictator	refugees

```
Q C S G H O E H S N C S K W I A P
T L E C S V V C O F O D W O K M V
Y C V Y T E L Q G L A I G O A U R
R R P W Z R M C Z K O I S C Q O J
E E V S N T E V W Y D C N A T Q I
Z W G U D H H Q U I S O A I V B E
S X K C Y R M K C Y I X A U A N S
E R A T I O N T T T R R K T S E I
E Z W J U W A Z A Q T X R G N T O
G D M Y D T B R E T A R G I M E E
U Z V V O S T E J G M R M H Q W L
F A O R W N D C F Q Y H B F J G V
E W L U E A N T I S E M I T I S M
R F G C X W W Z C M P A L K C A D
E L N G Y N H G L X D G G H R O W
K O U D K V K W W T U K L T C X C
C V C M P S H K P Q A D A X B V Q
```

100% Curriculum Vocabulary—Grades 6-12

3 Definitions — History

1. **boycott** — refusal to buy or sell something as a way to protest and/or force a change

2. **colonies** — areas of land settled and ruled by people from a distant country

3. **depression** — a bad economic period when companies decrease production and many people lose their jobs

4. **Dust Bowl** — part of the Great Plains that was severely damaged in the 1930s due to dust storms caused by the lack of rain

5. **expansion** — the result of people occupying increasing amounts of land

6. **forty-niners** — people who went to California to mine for gold during the 1849 gold rush

7. **loyalists** — American colonists who remained loyal to the British during the Revolutionary War

8. **Prohibition** — a time when it was against the law to make, sell, or possess alcoholic beverages

9. **truce** — an agreement by two countries, groups, or people to stop fighting

10. **wagon train** — a line of wagons that carried people who were traveling to the West

3 Fill-in-the-Blank — History

Fill in the blanks with the words or phrases from the box.

| boycott | Prohibition | forty-niners | Dust Bowl | truce |
| expansion | colonies | depression | loyalists | wagon train |

1. An agreement to stop fighting is a _____.

2. _____ were American colonists who remained loyal to the British.

3. Gold diggers during the 1849 gold rush were called _____.

4. People refusing to buy or sell as a way of protesting is a _____.

5. The _____ is part of the Great Plains that was severely damaged during the 1930 dust storms.

6. A bad economic period when companies decrease production and many people lose their jobs is a _____.

7. Many settlers who were traveling to the West went as part of a _____.

8. No one was allowed to drink or sell alcoholic beverages during _____.

9. _____ is the result of people occupying increasing amounts of land.

10. _____ are lands settled and ruled by people from a distant country.

3 Word Association — History

Write the word or phrase from the box next to the word or phrase that shares a similar meaning.

| boycott | Prohibition | forty-niners | Dust Bowl | truce |
| expansion | colonies | depression | loyalists | wagon train |

1. alcoholic beverages not allowed _____

2. agreement to stop fighting _____

3. bad economic period _____

4. Great Plains in the 1930s _____

5. protesting by refusing _____

6. line of wagons _____

7. people loyal to the British _____

8. areas of settled land _____

9. gold rush _____

10. occupying increasing amounts of land _____

3 Writing Sentences — History

Write a sentence using each word or phrase.

1. boycott

2. colonies

3. depression

4. Dust Bowl

5. expansion

6. forty-niners

7. loyalists

8. Prohibition

9. truce

10. wagon train

3 Crossword Puzzle — History

Complete the puzzle with words that match the clues.

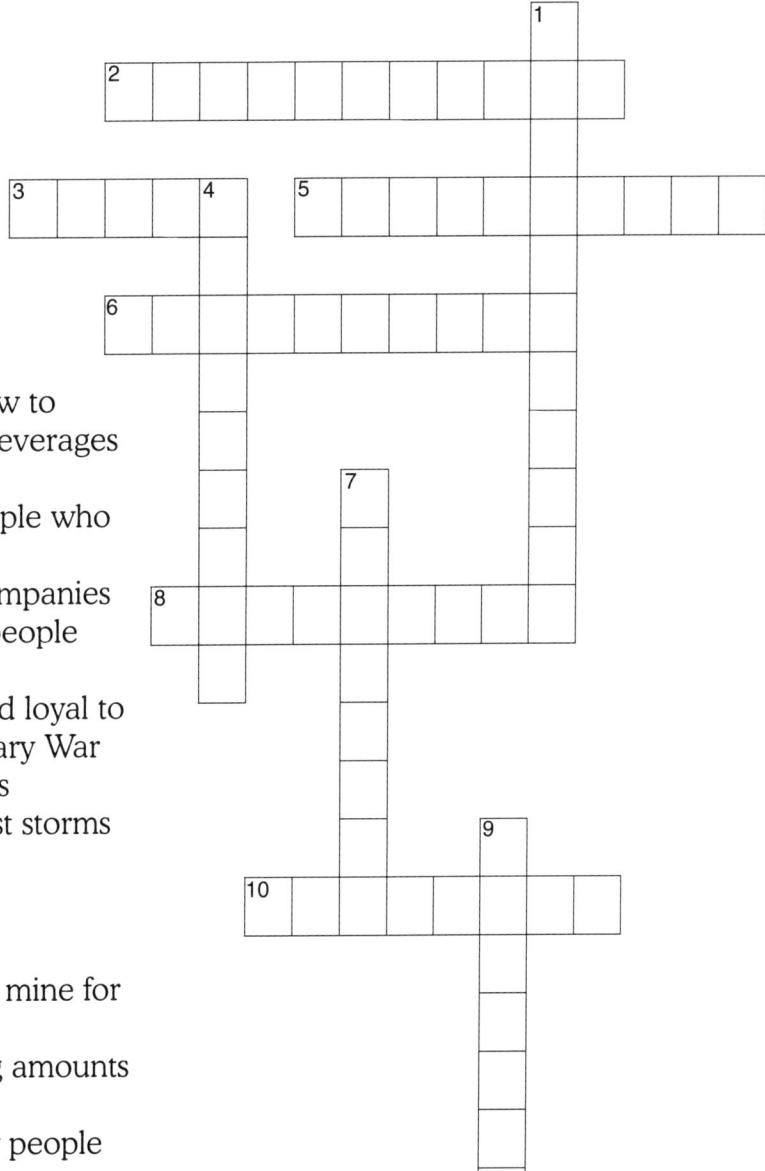

Across

2. a time when it was against the law to make, sell, or possess alcoholic beverages
3. an agreement to stop fighting
5. a line of wagons that carried people who were traveling to the West
6. a bad economic period when companies decrease production and many people lose their jobs
8. American colonists who remained loyal to the British during the Revolutionary War
10. a part of the Great Plains that was damaged in the 1930s due to dust storms caused by lack of rain

Down

1. people who went to California to mine for gold during the 1849 gold rush
4. the result of occupying increasing amounts of land
7. areas of land settled and ruled by people from a distant country
9. people refusing to buy or sell something as a way to protest and/or force a change

③ Word Search — History

All the words or phrases listed in the box appear in the puzzle — horizontally, vertically, diagonally, or backward. Find and circle them.

boycott	Prohibition	forty-niners	Dust Bowl	truce
expansion	colonies	depression	loyalists	wagon train

```
N C N B S R E N I N Y T R O F
P O I W G U R J I O N L F M D
L H I W E X P A N S I O N U H
S O T T I N R G Q H B V S S Z
G I Y A I T N X E T L T A D F
I Q P A N B O I U F B C J S Q
S Z Y O L E I X H O L O S H J
Z W G S S I S H W F O L X Q J
R A S P V Z S L O Y B O I I T
W N L K I K E T A R L N L Q A
E W E Y V F R B S T P I H L P
Q C K I V P P V D D K E F R P
C H U K D V E I V I Y S B L G
K Q K R N D D T T O C Y O B V
Y X D O T S U I V M A C M F G
```

100% Curriculum Vocabulary—Grades 6-12 Copyright © 2002 LinguiSystems, Inc.

① Definitions — Keyboarding

1. **Backspace** — a key that moves the cursor back one space at a time; it also erases characters

2. **Caps Lock** — the key that capitalizes all letters

3. **Control** — a key that does nothing all by itself but when pressed with another key or keys, it changes the normal effect of that key

4. **Enter** — a key that moves the cursor down to the next line and enters in system commands; also called the *return key*

5. **Escape** — the key that is used to cancel a function or exit part of a program

6. **Insert** — a key that is used to add or place a word, sentence, or paragraph into text

7. **keyboard** — a device attached to a computer that has a set of keys in rows with letters and numbers on them (When the keys are pushed, the letters or numbers appear on the screen.)

8. **Shift** — a key that capitalizes a letter when pressed with that letter key

9. **Tab** — a key that moves the cursor to a preset place

10. **word processing** — the act of typing documents on a computer with the ability to change, add to, or reprint a document without retyping it

1 Fill-in-the-Blank — Keyboarding

Fill in the blanks with the words or phrases from the box.

Backspace	Escape	word processing	Control	Shift
Enter	Caps Lock	keyboard	Insert	Tab

1. The _____ key moves the cursor to a preset place.

2. A key that moves the cursor down to the next line is the _____ key.

3. The key that capitalizes all letters is the _____ key.

4. Typing letters and other documents on a computer is called _____.

5. Press the _____ key to capitalize a letter.

6. A key that moves the cursor back one space at a time is the _____ key.

7. The _____ key is used to place a word, sentence, or paragraph into text.

8. The _____ key is used to cancel a function or exit part of a program.

9. A _____ is a device attached to a computer that has a set of keys in rows with letters and numbers on them.

10. The _____ key does nothing all by itself but when pressed with another key or keys, it changes the effect of that key.

1 Word Association — Keyboarding

Write the word or phrase from the box next to the word or phrase that shares a similar meaning.

Backspace	Escape	word processing	Control	Shift
Enter	Caps Lock	keyboard	Insert	Tab

1. set of keys _____

2. act of typing documents _____

3. key used to exit/cancel _____

4. return key _____

5. moves cursor to preset place _____

6. key that changes effect of key _____

7. key to add to text _____

8. key to move back one space _____

9. key to capitalize all letters _____

10. key used to capitalize _____

1 Writing Sentences — Keyboarding

Write a sentence using each word or phrase.

1. Backspace

2. Caps Lock

3. Control

4. Enter

5. Escape

6. Insert

7. keyboard

8. Shift

9. Tab

10. word processing

Crossword Puzzle — Keyboarding

Complete the puzzle with words that match the clues.

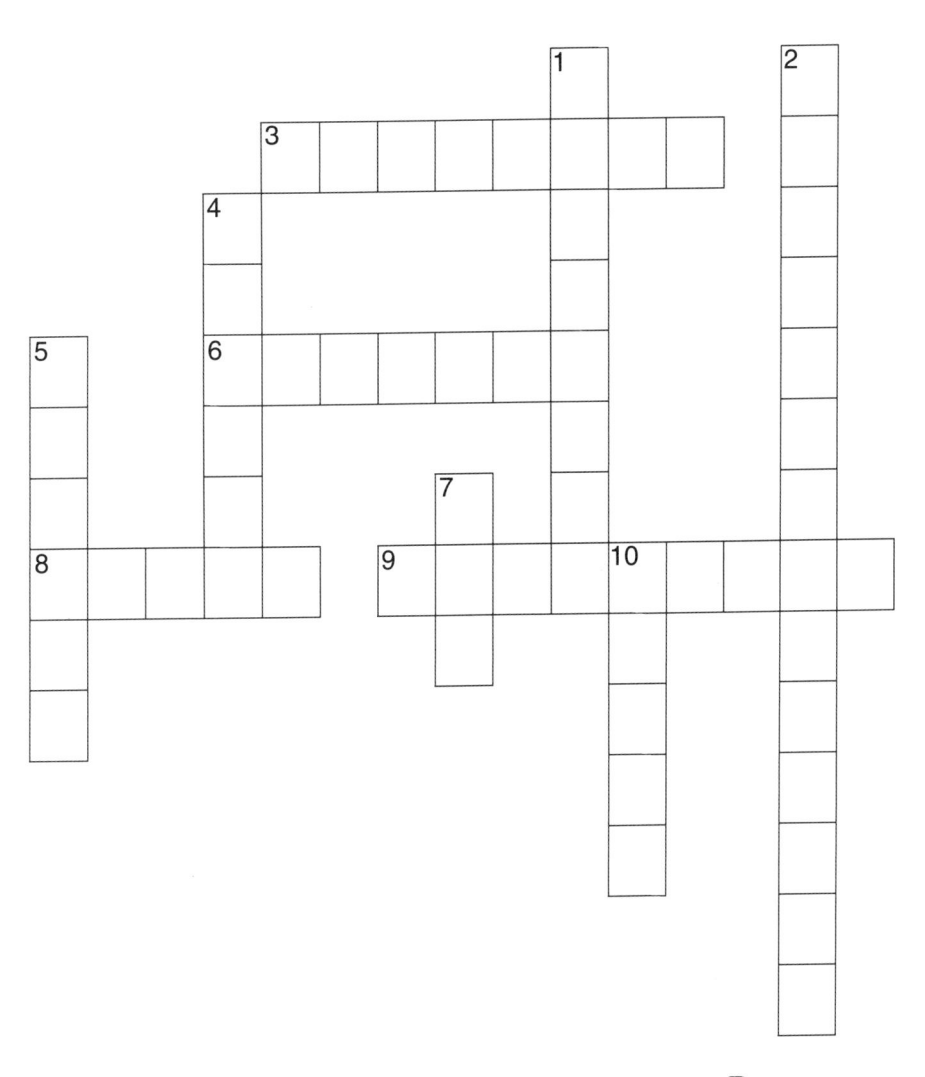

Across

3. a device with a set of keys in rows
6. the key that, when pressed with another key, changes the normal effect of that key
8. the key that moves the cursor down to the next line
9. the key that moves the cursor back one space at a time; also erases text

Down

1. the key that capitalizes all letters
2. the act of typing documents on a computer with the ability to change, add to, or reprint a document
4. the key that is used to cancel a function or exit part of a program
5. the key that is used to add or place a word, sentence, or paragraph into text
7. the key to move the cursor to a preset place
10. the key that capitalizes a letter when pressed with that letter

1 Word Search — Keyboarding

All the words or phrases listed in the box appear in the puzzle — horizontally, vertically, diagonally, or backward. Find and circle them.

| Backspace | Escape | word processing | Control | Shift |
| Enter | Caps Lock | keyboard | Insert | Tab |

```
W P X F B W L C C B E N T E R
N O S P Q X A V S A C F T S P
A U R C J P H X S C E R H V D
L E W D S E E H T K E K C C Y
L P N L P K U Y F S B T H L R
F A O L S R I J N P D L Z Q Q
Z C K P O H O I S A H A E S M
K S J P H R I C L C P Y N D O
E E W G B H T F E E Q X O U O
W O K W S A B N T S D Q J Z X
D R A O B Y E K O B S B F T H
V M K T K S Q K T C C I Q A G
U M I Y S D L O E T M X N B C
S Z R E M X J E Q I X G N G N
Z K X Y J M D X O C G D P A Q
```

100% Curriculum Vocabulary—Grades 6-12

② Definitions — Keyboarding

1. **accuracy** — a measurement of the number of words a person can type correctly

2. **delete** — to remove a letter, word, paragraph, etc., from a document

3. **directory** — a list of all the documents saved on a computer or a computer disk

4. **error** — a mistake

5. **indent** — to move the text farther to the right than the left margin (The first line of a paragraph is often indented.)

6. **print** — to produce a paper copy of a document that is on the computer screen

7. **retrieve** — a function that recovers information that has been saved

8. **save** — a function that records information on a disk, CD, or hard drive

9. **search** — a function that locates words or documents

10. **word wrap** — the automatic movement of a word to the next line when the word is too long to fit

2 Fill-in-the-Blank — Keyboarding

Fill in the blanks with the words or phrases from the box.

| accuracy | word wrap | error | save | print |
| search | delete | retrieve | directory | indent |

1. A function that records information on a disk, CD, or hard drive is the _____ function.

2. Use the _____ function to locate a word or document.

3. Writers often _____ the first line of a paragraph.

4. A _____ is a list of all the documents saved on a computer.

5. An _____ is a mistake.

6. When you _____ a page, you produce a paper copy of the document that is on the computer screen.

7. You measure a person's typing _____ by the number of words typed correctly.

8. To remove a letter or word from a document is to _____ it.

9. Use the _____ function to recover information that has been saved.

10. The automatic movement of a word to the next line is a _____.

100% Curriculum Vocabulary—Grades 6-12   Copyright © 2002 LinguiSystems, Inc.

② Word Association — Keyboarding

Write the word or phrase from the box next to the word or phrase that shares a similar meaning.

| accuracy | word wrap | error | save | print |
| search | delete | retrieve | directory | indent |

1. move text to the right _____

2. record information _____

3. mistake _____

4. automatically move to next line _____

5. list of files _____

6. recover _____

7. measurement of words typed correctly _____

8. to make a paper copy _____

9. remove _____

10. locate _____

2 Writing Sentences — Keyboarding

Write a sentence using each word or phrase.

1. accuracy

2. delete

3. directory

4. error

5. indent

6. print

7. retrieve

8. save

9. search

10. word wrap

Crossword Puzzle — Keyboarding

Complete the puzzle with words that match the clues.

Across

3. the automatic movement of a word to the next line
7. a function that recovers information that has been saved
10. a list of all the documents saved on a computer or computer disk

Down

1. a function that locates words or documents
2. to remove a letter or word from a document
4. a measurement of the number of words a person can type correctly
5. to move the text farther to the right than the left margin
6. a function that records information on a disk, CD, or hard drive
8. a mistake
9. to produce a paper copy of a document that is on the computer screen

② Word Search — Keyboarding

All the words or phrases listed in the box appear in the puzzle — horizontally, vertically, diagonally, or backward. Find and circle them.

accuracy	word wrap	error	save	print
search	delete	retrieve	directory	indent

```
A E D F P R Q D H N O K M W F
H Z Z O X M E C O B X K L O F
D C C J Q K R T T R X N S R M
B R R W O K C N R I F O L D R
H R M A A U I M A I N Y J W O
S W B D E R S A V E E N H R R
G B F Y P S M K Y T F V H A R
Z Y Z M M M J R K N D M E P E
A D E V U D O T C H B Y M H T
Y J D B E T A P P O E M Y N J
X A O L C P I P L M L B A C R
G U E E A C C U R A C Y W J S
J T R W S X T N E D N I E J M
E I B U Q M V C V T T W L L F
D R P S O V A Y N X X D U E H
```

3 Definitions — Keyboarding

1. **backup copy** — a second copy or duplicate of a document or program that is written on a disk or CD

2. **bold** — letters shown thicker and darker

3. **centering** — placing text in the middle of a line with equal space on both sides

4. **cursor** — a blinking box or line on the screen that shows where the next letter, number, or space will be placed

5. **double space** — to press the Enter key twice to create one blank line between each line of text

6. **format** — the arrangement, placement, and spacing of the text and pictures within a document

7. **header/footer** — information typed onto the top/bottom margin of a sheet of paper such as the title of the document, page number, or date

8. **margin** — the part of a page outside the main body of text; includes the right, left, top, and bottom of the document

9. **printer** — a machine attached to a computer that can print a paper copy

10. **single space** — to press the Enter key once so there are no blank lines between lines of text

3 Fill-in-the-Blank — Keyboarding

Fill in the blanks with the words or phrases from the box.

bold	header/footer	double space	centering	margin
cursor	backup copy	printer	format	single space

1. The part of a page outside the main body of text is the _____.

2. A second copy, or duplicate, of a document is a _____.

3. Pressing the Enter key twice so there is a blank line between each line of text is creating a _____.

4. Pressing the Enter key once so there are no blank lines between lines of text is creating a _____.

5. A machine attached to the computer that can print a paper copy is a _____.

6. _____ is placing text in the middle of a line.

7. A _____ is a blinking line on the screen that shows where the next letter or space will be placed.

8. A _____ is typed onto the top/bottom margin of the paper and contains information such as the title, page number, or date.

9. A _____ letter is thicker and darker than others.

10. The _____ of a document is the arrangement, placement, and spacing of text and pictures.

Word Association — Keyboarding

Write the word or phrase from the box next to the word or phrase that shares a similar meaning.

bold	header/footer	double space	centering	margin
cursor	backup copy	printer	format	single space

1. one blank line between text _____

2. arrangement of text and pictures _____

3. no blank lines between text _____

4. machine that can print _____

5. thick and dark _____

6. blinking line _____

7. duplicate file _____

8. title, page number, or date _____

9. right, left, top, or bottom _____

10. placing text in the middle _____

3 Writing Sentences — Keyboarding

Write a sentence using each word or phrase.

1. backup copy

2. bold

3. centering

4. cursor

5. double space

6. format

7. header/footer

8. margin

9. printer

10. single space

Crossword Puzzle 3 — Keyboarding

Complete the puzzle with words that match the clues.

Across

5. a machine attached to a computer that can print a paper copy
6. letters that are thick and dark
7. placing text in the middle of a line
8. a duplicate of a document or program that is written on a disk
9. information typed onto the top or bottom margin of a paper such as the title, page number, or date

Down

1. to press the Enter key twice to create one blank line between each line of text
2. to press the Enter key once so there are no blank lines between text lines
3. the part of a page outside the main body of text
4. a blinking box or line on the screen that shows where the next letter, number, or space will be placed
10. the arrangement, placing, and spacing text within a document

③ Word Search — Keyboarding

All the words or phrases listed in the box appear in the puzzle — horizontally, vertically, diagonally, or backward. Find and circle them.

bold	header/footer	double space	centering	margin
cursor	backup copy	printer	format	single space

```
R E T O O F R E D A E H Y V G
P F C E N T E R I N G P C T U
Z R V A T N F X Z N O Q H P O
C Q I Z P O P W U C I J E F B
E M M N R S S R P N I G R A M
C Q W M T Z E U R F S B A U O
A I A H D E K L G F Y N C J B
P T T C W C R F B R O X U E W
S D A J A U W N Z U X Y R D V
E K M B X Y D J H Y O Y S Q P
L A F U D O W N P J D D O T W
G R Z J Y L Z U W V K L R O E
N K M O B C O S F G M D K P E
I Z I W J W T B O S R Z F A D
S N U S B Y J U N Q E Y Q H U
```

100% Curriculum Vocabulary—Grades 6-12

Definitions — Math

1. **angle** — the space or distance between two lines that meet

2. **arc** — a part of a circle

3. **bisect** — to divide a line, angle, or arc into two equal parts

4. **circumference** — the distance around a circle

5. **congruent** — having the same size or shape

6. **diameter** — a line that passes through the center of a circle and has both endpoints on the circle

7. **geometry** — the study of shapes, sizes, and properties of figures

8. **parallel lines** — two lines that are always the same distance apart and never intersect

9. **perimeter** — the distance around the outside of something such as a building

10. **tangent** — a line that touches a curve or surface in a single point but does not go through it

① Fill-in-the-Blank — Math

Fill in the blanks with the words or phrases from the box.

| bisect | perimeter | circumference | parallel lines | arc |
| tangent | diameter | angle | congruent | geometry |

1. The distance around a circle is the _____.

2. An _____ is the space or distance between two lines that meet.

3. A line that passes through the center of a circle is the _____.

4. The _____ is the distance around the outside of something.

5. Two figures that are the same size and shape are _____.

6. _____ is the study of shapes, sizes, and properties of figures.

7. Two lines that are always the same distance apart are _____.

8. When you _____ a line or angle, you divide it into two equal parts.

9. A line that touches a curve but does not go through it is a _____.

10. An _____ is a part of a circle.

100% Curriculum Vocabulary—Grades 6-12   254   Copyright © 2002 LinguiSystems, Inc.

① Word Association — Math

Write the word or phrase from the box next to the word or phrase that shares a similar meaning.

| bisect | perimeter | circumference | parallel lines | arc |
| tangent | diameter | angle | congruent | geometry |

1. distance around a circle _____

2. the study of shapes _____

3. distance between two lines that meet _____

4. lines that never intersect _____

5. divide into equal parts _____

6. line touching a single point _____

7. same size and shape _____

8. distance around the outside of something _____

9. part of a circle _____

10. line through the center of a circle _____

100% Curriculum Vocabulary—Grades 6-12   Copyright © 2002 LinguiSystems, Inc.

1 Writing Sentences — Math

Write a sentence using each word or phrase.

1. angle

2. arc

3. bisect

4. circumference

5. congruent

6. diameter

7. geometry

8. parallel lines

9. perimeter

10. tangent

Crossword Puzzle — Math

Complete the puzzle with words that match the clues.

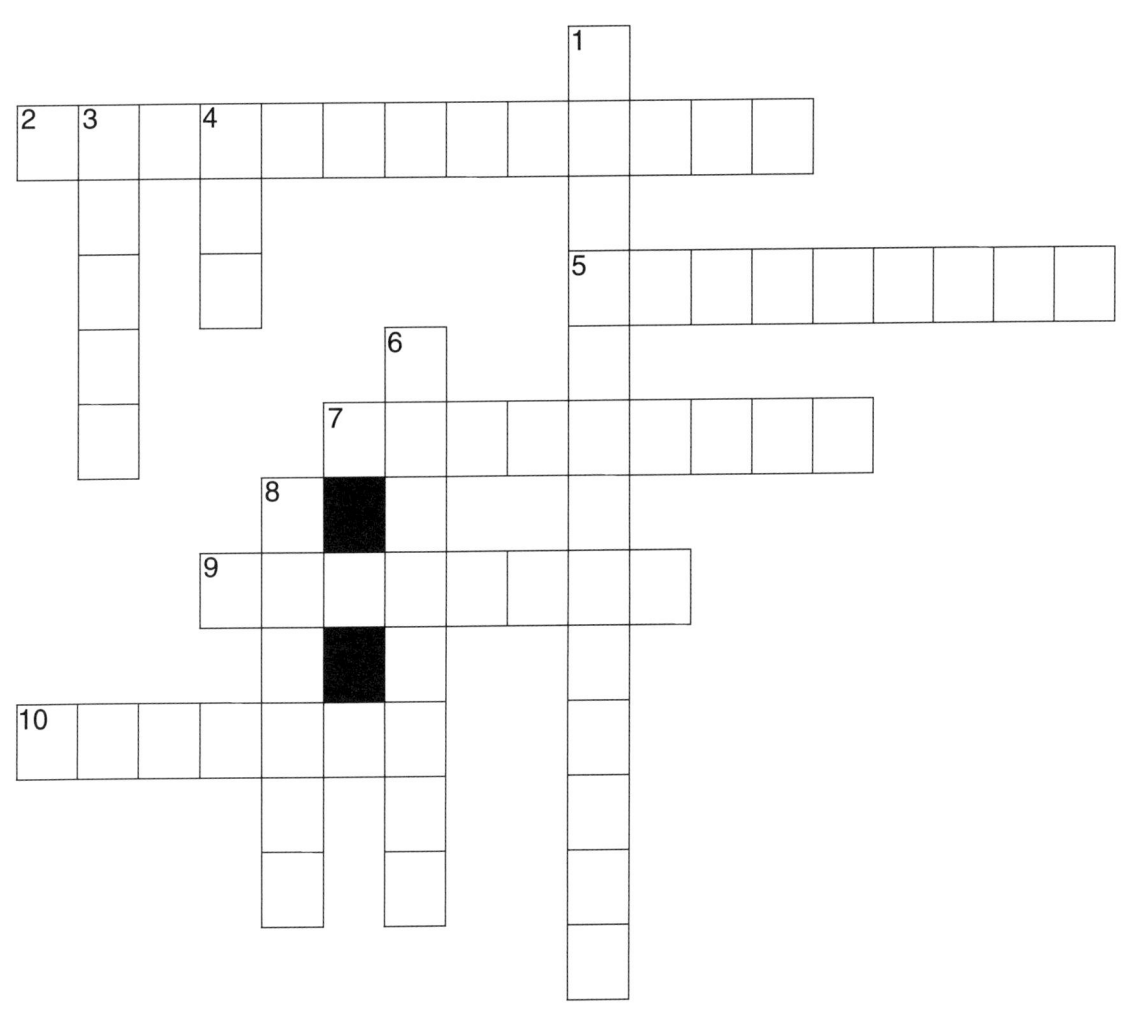

Across

2. two lines that are always the same distance apart and never intersect
5. having the same size or shape
7. the distance around the outside of something
9. a line that passes through the center of a circle and has both endpoints on the circle
10. a line that touches a curve or surface in a single point but does not go through it

Down

1. the distance around a circle
3. the space or distance between two lines that meet
4. a part of a circle
6. the study of shapes, sizes, and properties of figures
8. to divide a line, angle, or arc into two equal parts

1 Word Search — Math

All the words or phrases listed in the box appear in the puzzle — horizontally, vertically, diagonally, or backward. Find and circle them.

bisect	perimeter	circumference	parallel lines	arc
tangent	diameter	angle	congruent	geometry

```
Q P G T U Q B G G U T X E J X
C W E U N E X E A R C C N R K
X C I R L E O L C W N O T U Q
C P N G I M G Z P E M N C U F
T Z N Y E M V N R X W G E X R
P A F T P J E E A I V R S T K
X H R E X I F T O T W U I M A
M Y F M F M N N E N M E B Y V
A S C Y U I H A M R W N G U L
P W G C F Z X S K B W T K R G
P A R A L L E L L I N E S O U
L I R E T E M A I D N F Z T E
C S B A G I D J P J A B T J V
G R M C U A W D O K Q G Z C Z
W L B K H O T G B H V U M E Q
```

② Definitions — Math

1. **compass** — an instrument used to draw circles or arcs

2. **decrease** — to make smaller

3. **denominator** — the number below the line in a fraction

4. **dividend** — the number that is divided in a division problem

5. **division** — a math process used to find out how many times a number is contained in another number

6. **fraction** — a number with a numerator and a denominator that names a part of a whole

7. **increase** — to make larger

8. **numerator** — the number above the line in a fraction

9. **percent** — a ratio that compares a number to 100; written as %

10. **protractor** — an instrument used to measure angles

2 Fill-in-the-Blank — Math

Fill in the blanks with the words from the box.

decrease	division	fraction	numerator	denominator
percent	protractor	compass	dividend	increase

1. To make something smaller is to _____ it.

2. The number below the line in a fraction is the _____.

3. A _____ is a ratio that compares a number to 100.

4. A math process used to find out how many times a number is contained in another number is _____.

5. To _____ something is to make it larger.

6. A number with a numerator and a denominator is a _____.

7. A _____ is an instrument used to measure angles.

8. The number that is divided in a division problem is the _____.

9. A _____ is an instrument used to draw circles or arcs.

10. The number above the line in a fraction is the _____.

② Word Association — Math

Write the word from the box next to the word or phrase that shares a similar meaning.

| decrease | division | fraction | numerator | denominator |
| percent | protractor | compass | dividend | increase |

1. used to draw circles _____
2. bottom number of fraction _____
3. not a whole number _____
4. measures angles _____
5. to make smaller _____
6. number divided _____
7. math process _____
8. to make larger _____
9. top number of fraction _____
10. % _____

2 Writing Sentences — Math

Write a sentence using each word.

1. compass

2. decrease

3. denominator

4. dividend

5. division

6. fraction

7. increase

8. numerator

9. percent

10. protractor

100% Curriculum Vocabulary—Grades 6-12

Crossword Puzzle — Math

Complete the puzzle with words that match the clues.

Across

3. an instrument used to draw circles or arcs
4. a ratio that compares a number to 100; written as %
7. the number above the line in a fraction
8. to make smaller
9. a number with a numerator and a denominator that names a part of a whole
10. the number below the line in a fraction

Down

1. to make larger
2. the number that is divided in a division problem
5. an instrument used to measure angles
6. a math process used to find out how many times a number is contained in another number

② Word Search — Math

All the words or phrases listed in the box appear in the puzzle — horizontally, vertically, diagonally, or backward. Find and circle them.

decrease	division	fraction	numerator	denominator
percent	protractor	compass	dividend	increase

```
I P F Y E Y F W N X K Y F I P
D W E O Q J D U O V Z E I Q R
N E X R O C M B I S U M U E O
U V N K C E J G T M L J I P T
R I R O R E Y L C W V G K N R
D O F A M J N J A X T J B I A
Q N T S X I X T R K V O E C C
J O E I S K N N F S C S W O T
R T Q D S F G A O U A K R M O
N O I S I V I D T E R U N P R
Z O V S X V H Z R O I I M A J
T M F J F P I C K R U S S P
W O K X E B N D E C R E A S E
T L A K I I C A T K T V H I T
T D M P P T E V Y P A K L W G
```

100% Curriculum Vocabulary—Grades 6-12

3 Definitions — Math

1. **addition** — a math process where two or more numbers are added to get a sum

2. **algebra** — a type of math that uses letters to represent numbers to solve problems

3. **bar graph** — a graph using bars of different lengths or heights to show and compare data

4. **coordinates** — a pair of numbers that locates a point

5. **decimal** — a number with one or more digits to the right of the decimal point (e.g., 2.45)

6. **equation** — a math sentence with an equal sign (=)

7. **even number** — a whole number that is a multiple of two

8. **integer** — any positive or negative whole number, including zero

9. **line graph** — a graph that uses a line to show changes over a period of time

10. **negative number** — a number less than zero (e.g., -5)

3 Fill-in-the-Blank — Math

Fill in the blanks with the words or phrases from the box.

algebra	negative number	coordinates	line graph	equation
integer	addition	even number	decimal	bar graph

1. A pair of numbers that locates a point are _____.

2. An _____ is a whole number that is a multiple of two.

3. The type of math that uses letters for numbers is _____.

4. A _____ uses a line to show changes over a period of time.

5. A number less than zero is a _____.

6. An _____ is a math sentence with an equal sign.

7. A _____ uses bars of different lengths and heights to show and compare data.

8. An _____ is any positive or negative whole number.

9. The number 7.25 is a _____.

10. _____ is a math process where two or more numbers are added to get a sum.

100% Curriculum Vocabulary—Grades 6-12

3. Word Association — Math

Write the word or phrase from the box next to the word or phrase that shares a similar meaning.

algebra	negative number	coordinates	line graph	equation
integer	addition	even number	decimal	bar graph

1. can be divided by two _____

2. uses a line to show changes _____

3. 0, 3, or -9 _____

4. math process used to get a sum _____

5. locates a point _____

6. a math sentence _____

7. graph with bars _____

8. 5.28 _____

9. less than zero _____

10. uses letters for numbers _____

3 Writing Sentences — Math

Write a sentence using each word or phrase.

1. addition

2. algebra

3. bar graph

4. coordinates

5. decimal

6. equation

7. even number

8. integer

9. line graph

10. negative number

100% Curriculum Vocabulary—Grades 6-12

Crossword Puzzle — Math

Complete the puzzle with words that match the clues.

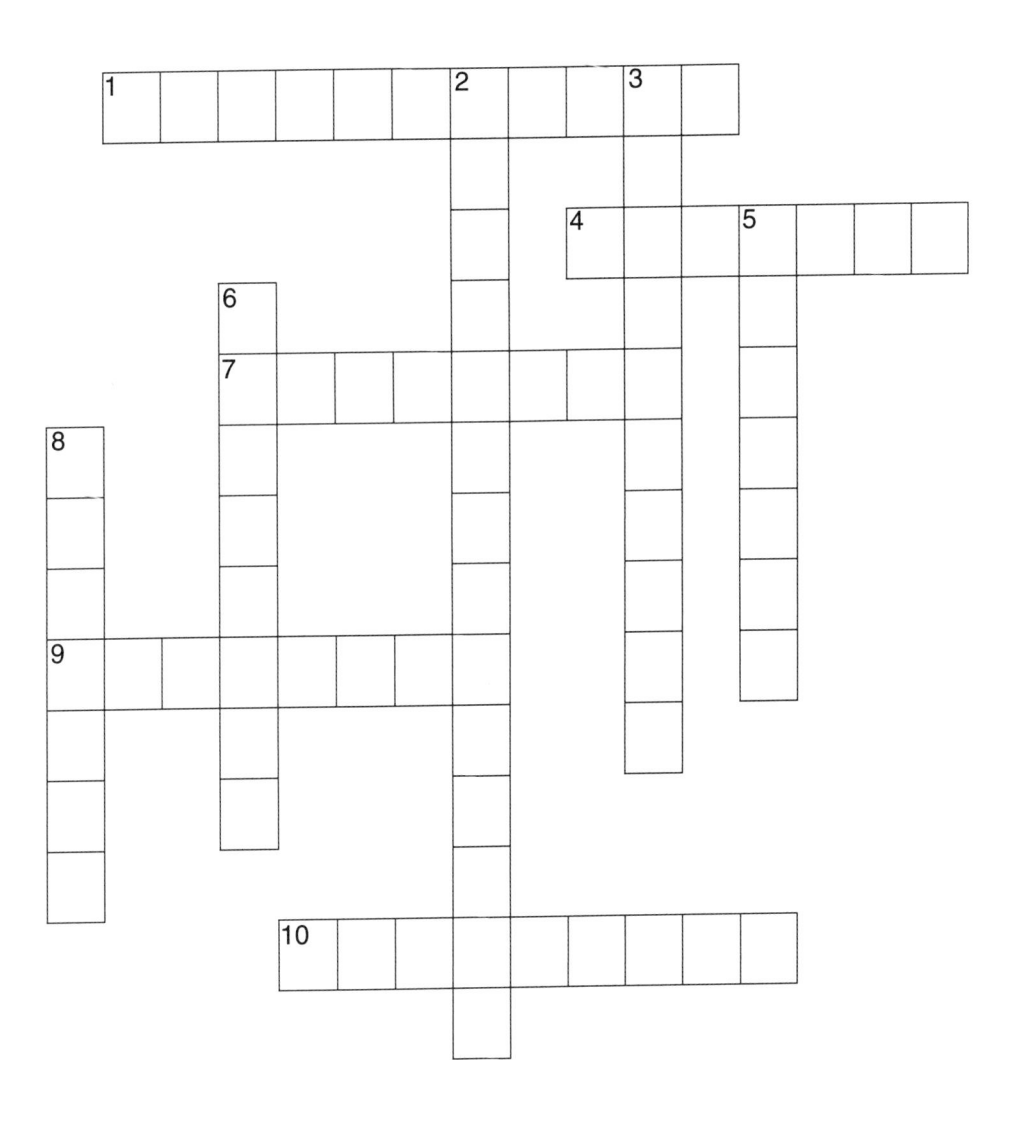

Across

1. a pair of numbers that locates a point
4. a number with one or more digits to the right of the decimal point
7. adding two or more numbers to get a sum
9. a math sentence with an equal sign (=)
10. a graph that uses a line to show changes over a period of time

Down

2. a number less than zero
3. a whole number that is a multiple of two
5. any positive or negative whole number, including zero
6. a graph using bars of different lengths or heights to show and compare data
8. a type of math that uses letters to represent numbers to solve problems

③ Word Search — Math

All the words or phrases listed in the box appear in the puzzle — horizontally, vertically, diagonally, or backward. Find and circle them.

algebra	negative number	coordinates	line graph	equation
integer	addition	even number	decimal	bar graph

```
V R V L U A I I L J E J S A H
K E P M I R R A E Q N E I D U
O B R H A N M B U E T V W D S
L M U A R I E A E A U Q I I J
W U Z P C X T G N G Q A V T M
K N M E G I R I R O L B P I S
K E D S O K D H D A P A V O R
E V G N Z R O Q E O P A R N E
X I A W O S H R Q L H H P S G
A T K O V N H P A R G R A B E
L A C U W A F B P J C W Z W T
L G E V E N N U M B E R G T N
H E N O N B B O W G G U B K I
W N Z O S Q C N M V F I X H Y
W X K D S M S L N A G P A B T
```

100% Curriculum Vocabulary—Grades 6-12

4 Definitions — Math

1. **foot** — a measurement of length; 1 foot equals 12 inches

2. **gallon** — a liquid measurement that equals four quarts

3. **inch** — a small length of measurement; 12 inches equal 1 foot

4. **length** — a measured distance, usually in feet or inches

5. **pound** — a measurement of weight that is equal to 16 ounces

6. **quart** — a liquid measurement smaller than a gallon; four quarts equal one gallon

7. **review** — to look at or study again

8. **solution** — the answer to a problem

9. **volume** — the number of cubic units of space taken up by a solid

10. **yard** — a measurement of length that is equal to three feet

4 Fill-in-the-Blank — Math

Fill in the blanks with the words from the box.

foot	volume	inch	review	pound
yard	gallon	solution	length	quart

1. The answer to a problem is the _____.

2. A _____ is a measurement of length that is equal to 12 inches.

3. Students should _____ their notes before taking an exam.

4. An _____ is a length of measurement that is smaller than a foot.

5. _____ is the number of cubic units of space taken up by a solid.

6. One _____ equals 16 ounces.

7. The _____ of an object is usually measured in feet or inches.

8. Three feet are equal to one _____.

9. A _____ is a liquid measurement that equals four quarts.

10. A measurement of liquid smaller than a gallon is a _____.

4 Word Association — Math

Write the word from the box next to the word or phrase that shares a similar meaning.

> foot   volume   inch   review   pound
> yard   gallon   solution   length   quart

1. study again _____

2. equals 12 inches _____

3. equals four quarts _____

4. equals three feet _____

5. answer _____

6. liquid measurement smaller than a gallon _____

7. equals 16 ounces _____

8. cubic units of space _____

9. a small length of measurement _____

10. a measured distance _____

4 Writing Sentences — Math

Write a sentence using each word.

1. foot

2. gallon

3. inch

4. length

5. pound

6. quart

7. review

8. solution

9. volume

10. yard

Crossword Puzzle — Math

Complete the puzzle with words that match the clues.

Across

5. the number of cubic units of space taken up by a solid
6. a measurement of length that is equal to three feet
7. a measured distance, usually in feet or inches
9. the answer to a problem

Down

1. a measurement of length that equals 12 inches
2. a measurement of weight that is equal to 16 ounces
3. to look at or study again
4. a measurement of liquid smaller than one gallon
8. a liquid measurement that equals four quarts
10. a small length of measurement; 12 equal 1 foot

4 Word Search — Math

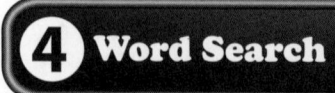

All the words or phrases listed in the box appear in the puzzle — horizontally, vertically, diagonally, or backward. Find and circle them.

foot	volume	inch	review	pound
yard	gallon	solution	length	quart

```
H Q U A R T M D A I S R J C E
J T Z F H X N D S N O B E W G
T K G I T U Y C T C L C F M J
D L Y N O U U D Z H U H O E G
W F M P E V U Z T K T U B P X
G V C N O L L A G K I E D C M
U C D L C F D W H A O H Q A L
N R U P U R C E D Y N Z S V S
J M T J H G U I S F X Q W Q E
E S J M E K J V G K Z T Y E O
T A Y I I Z L E D N F W M E H
G M A J H Y B R Y O J G H R O
X B I D T Z K N O A W V N M L
B A L K A V H T H E R H L K R
R U C J L K R O F C A D T Q J
```

100% Curriculum Vocabulary—Grades 6-12

Answer Key

Art 1
(pages 19-24)

page 20
1. contrast
2. calligraphy
3. design
4. abstract
5. glaze
6. balanced
7. bright
8. contour
9. collage
10. Casting

page 21
1. bright
2. design
3. balanced
4. contrast
5. calligraphy
6. abstract
7. glaze
8. contour
9. casting
10. collage

page 22
Answers will vary.

page 23
Across
1. calligraphy
4. contour
5. balanced
7. casting
9. collage

Down
2. abstract
3. bright
4. contrast
6. design
8. glaze

page 24

Art 2
(pages 25-30)

page 26
1. pigment
2. hue
3. illusion
4. line
5. ceramics
6. pattern
7. texture
8. primary color
9. kiln
10. Perspective

page 27
1. pattern
2. primary color
3. pigment
4. illusion
5. line
6. kiln
7. texture
8. ceramics
9. hue
10. perspective

page 28
Answers will vary.

page 29
Across
1. pigment
5. kiln
7. texture
8. hue
9. primary color

Down
1. perspective
2. pattern
3. line
4. ceramics
6. illusion

page 30

Biology 1
(pages 31-36)

page 32
1. Lymph nodes
2. cornea
3. aorta
4. kidneys
5. lungs
6. colon
7. gall bladder
8. esophagus
9. organ
10. small intestine

page 33
1. small intestine
2. organ
3. gall bladder
4. lymph nodes
5. cornea
6. lungs
7. colon
8. esophagus
9. kidneys
10. aorta

page 34
Answers will vary.

page 35
Across
1. organ
3. lymph nodes
4. small intestine
5. kidneys
6. esophagus
8. cornea

Down
2. gall bladder
3. lungs
7. aorta
8. colon

page 36

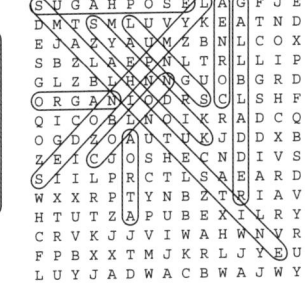

Biology 2
(pages 37-42)

page 38
1. recessive trait
2. mutation
3. gene
4. chromosomes
5. dominant trait
6. Mitosis
7. clone
8. traits
9. Meiosis
10. heredity

page 39
1. chromosomes
2. mitosis
3. dominant trait
4. heredity
5. mutation
6. meiosis
7. recessive trait
8. clone
9. gene
10. traits

page 40
Answers will vary.

page 41
Across
3. mitosis
5. heredity
6. gene
10. recessive trait

Down
1. traits
2. dominant trait
4. chromosomes
7. mutation
8. meiosis
9. clone

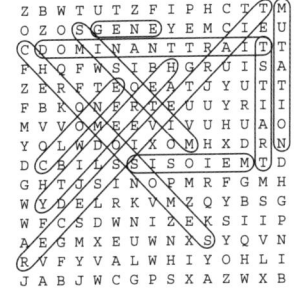

page 42

100% Curriculum Vocabulary—Grades 6-12   Copyright © 2002 LinguiSystems, Inc.

Answer Key, continued

Biology 3
(pages 43-48)

page 44
1. Bacteria
2. antigen
3. artery
4. Alveoli
5. antibiotics
6. antibody
7. marrow
8. capillary
9. clot
10. Immunity

page 45
1. antibiotics
2. clot
3. antibody
4. antigen
5. alveoli
6. capillary
7. bacteria
8. artery
9. immunity
10. marrow

page 46
Answers will vary.

page 47
Across
2. antibiotics
4. alveoli
7. antibody
8. artery
9. immunity

Down
1. capillary
3. bacteria
5. clot
6. marrow
8. antigen

page 48

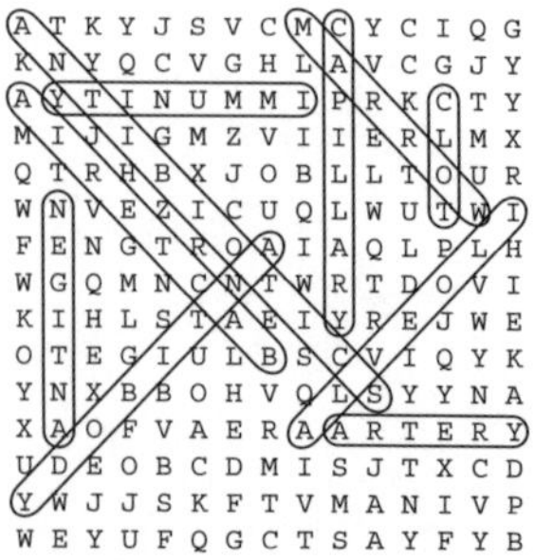

Biology 4
(pages 49-54)

page 50
1. venom
2. consumer
3. herbivore
4. decomposer
5. invertebrate
6. food chain
7. producer
8. parasite
9. carnivore
10. organism

page 51
1. carnivore
2. decomposer
3. organism
4. producer
5. herbivore
6. venom
7. invertebrate
8. food chain
9. consumer
10. parasite

page 52
Answers will vary.

page 53
Across
2. food chain
6. decomposer
7. venom
9. herbivore
10. parasite

Down
1. invertebrate
3. carnivore
4. producer
5. consumer
8. organism

page 54

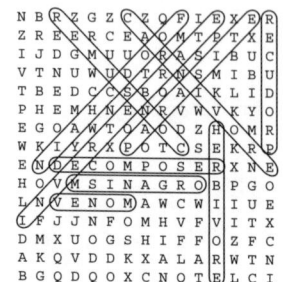

Biology 5
(pages 55-60)

page 56
1. joint
2. anterior
3. cartilage
4. molecule
5. central nervous system
6. virus
7. element
8. embryo
9. disease
10. posterior

page 57
1. central nervous system
2. cartilage
3. disease
4. element
5. embryo
6. joint
7. anterior
8. molecule
9. posterior
10. virus

page 58
Answers will vary.

page 59
Across
3. joint
9. virus
10. central nervous system

Down
1. cartilage
2. posterior
4. anterior
5. molecule
6. element
7. embryo
8. disease

page 60

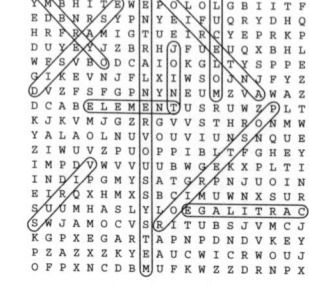

Consumer 1
(pages 61-66)

page 62
1. checking account
2. withhold
3. expenditure
4. Biweekly
5. gross pay
6. balance
7. adjust
8. net pay
9. salary
10. interest

page 63
1. balance
2. biweekly
3. withhold
4. salary
5. expenditure
6. gross pay
7. interest
8. net pay
9. checking account
10. adjust

page 64
Answers will vary.

page 65
Across
4. salary
6. biweekly
8. net pay
9. checking account

Down
1. gross pay
2. expenditure
3. interest
5. withhold
7. balance
10. adjust

page 66

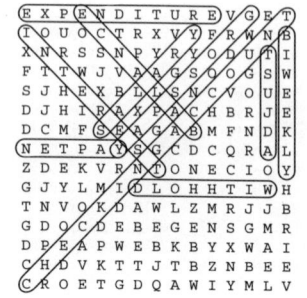

100% Curriculum Vocabulary—Grades 6-12

Answer Key, continued

Consumer 2
(pages 67-72)

page 68
1. promotion
2. company
3. schedule
4. address
5. interview
6. time card
7. résumé
8. employee
9. position
10. application

page 69
1. position
2. promotion
3. address
4. employee
5. company
6. application
7. résumé
8. schedule
9. time card
10. interview

page 70
Answers will vary.

page 71
Across
6. promotion
7. interview
9. résumé
10. employee

Down
1. position
2. application
3. company
4. time card
5. address
8. schedule

page 72

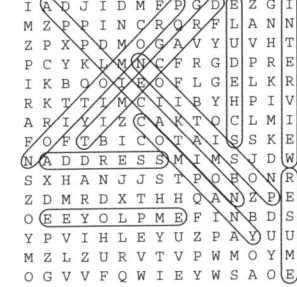

Consumer 3
(pages 73-78)

page 74
1. identification
2. sale price
3. rent
4. discount
5. credit card
6. lease
7. odds
8. mortgage
9. advertisement
10. mean

page 75
1. mean
2. lease
3. rent
4. odds
5. identification
6. mortgage
7. discount
8. credit card
9. advertisement
10. sale price

page 76
Answers will vary.

page 77
Across
3. lease
5. mean
6. advertisement
8. rent
9. mortgage

Down
1. credit card
2. identification
4. sale price
7. discount
10. odds

page 78

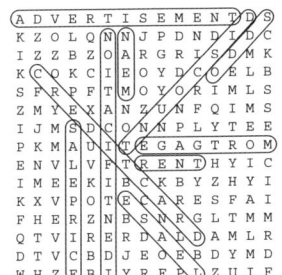

Consumer 4
(pages 79-84)

page 80
1. shoulder
2. restriction
3. lane
4. merge
5. pedestrian
6. visibility
7. residential
8. detour
9. prohibited
10. car pool

page 81
1. residential
2. merge
3. pedestrian
4. prohibited
5. shoulder
6. car pool
7. detour
8. restriction
9. visibility
10. lane

page 82
Answers will vary.

page 83
Across
1. pedestrian
4. visibility
7. car pool
9. detour
10. residential

Down
2. restriction
3. prohibited
5. merge
6. shoulder
8. lane

page 84

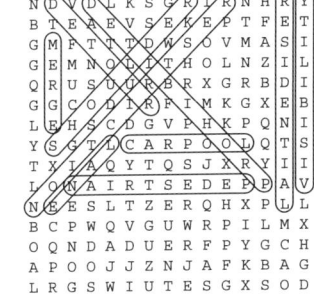

Earth Science 1
(pages 85-90)

page 86
1. Fahrenheit
2. tornado
3. Celsius
4. atmosphere
5. hurricane
6. Evaporation
7. saturated
8. barometer
9. precipitation
10. climate

page 87
1. evaporation
2. Celsius
3. climate
4. tornado
5. saturated
6. hurricane
7. atmosphere
8. Fahrenheit
9. barometer
10. precipitation

page 88
Answers will vary.

page 89
Across
1. evaporation
6. Fahrenheit
9. Celsius
10. climate

Down
2. precipitation
3. atmosphere
4. barometer
5. saturated
7. hurricane
8. tornado

page 90

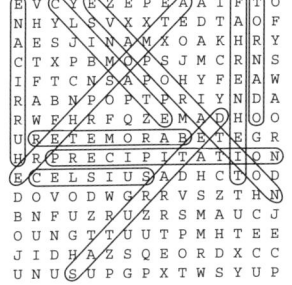

100% Curriculum Vocabulary—Grades 6-12   279   Copyright © 2002 LinguiSystems, Inc.

Answer Key, continued

Earth Science 2
(pages 91-96)

page 92
1. nebula
2. supernova
3. asteroid
4. orbit
5. black hole
6. meteor
7. galaxy
8. planet
9. constellation
10. astronomer

page 93
1. meteor
2. constellation
3. galaxy
4. astronomer
5. black hole
6. orbit
7. supernova
8. nebula
9. asteroid
10. planet

page 94
Answers will vary.

page 95
Across
4. meteor
5. astronomer
6. black hole
8. orbit
10. supernova

Down
1. nebula
2. planet
3. constellation
7. asteroid
9. galaxy

page 96

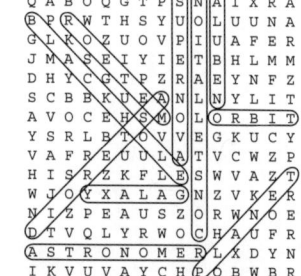

Earth Science 3
(pages 97-102)

page 98
1. pollen
2. deciduous
3. stamen
4. seed
5. pistil
6. roots
7. anther
8. photosynthesis
9. stem
10. Fruit

page 99
1. anther
2. deciduous
3. pistil
4. roots
5. stamen
6. pollen
7. photosynthesis
8. stem
9. fruit
10. seed

page 100
Answers will vary.

page 101
Across
1. stem
2. pistil
3. deciduous
5. roots
7. anther
8. stamen

Down
1. seed
2. photosynthesis
4. pollen
6. fruit

page 102

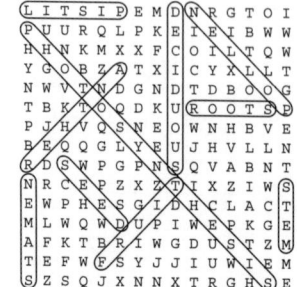

Earth Science 4
(pages 103-108)

page 104
1. crest
2. Erosion
3. pollutant
4. Irrigation
5. catalytic converter
6. cavern
7. delta
8. Acid rain
9. Desalination
10. alluvial fan

page 105
1. delta
2. desalination
3. cavern
4. irrigation
5. catalytic converter
6. erosion
7. acid rain
8. alluvial fan
9. pollutant
10. crest

page 106
Answers will vary.

page 107
Across
1. cavern
5. pollutant
6. crest
7. irrigation
10. desalination

Down
2. acid rain
3. catalytic converter
4. alluvial fan
8. erosion
9. delta

page 108

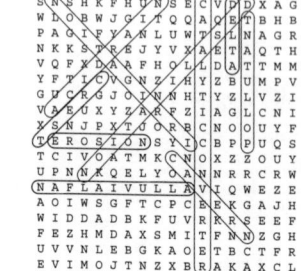

Earth Science 5
(pages 109-114)

page 110
1. Cenozoic era
2. epicenter
3. earthquake
4. glacier
5. Paleozoic era
6. Big Bang theory
7. Igneous rock
8. Precambrian era
9. iceberg
10. Mesozoic era

page 111
1. Big Bang theory
2. Cenozoic era
3. igneous rock
4. Paleozoic era
5. iceberg
6. earthquake
7. Precambrian era
8. epicenter
9. glacier
10. Mesozoic era

page 112
Answers will vary.

page 113
Across
2. Paleozoic era
4. Big Bang theory
7. Cenozoic era
8. igneous rock
9. iceberg

Down
1. epicenter
2. Precambrian era
3. earthquake
5. Mesozoic era
6. glacier

page 114

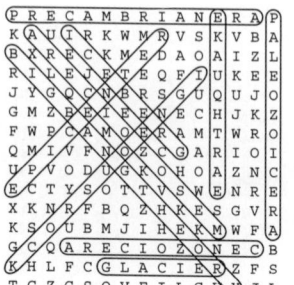

Answer Key, continued

Earth Science 6
(pages 115-120)

page 116
1. conservation
2. core
3. alloy
4. fossil
5. contract
6. element
7. Depletion
8. Fossil fuel
9. expand
10. Data

page 117
1. data
2. contract
3. depletion
4. fossil fuel
5. element
6. fossil
7. core
8. alloy
9. expand
10. conservation

page 118
Answers will vary.

page 119
Across
1. core
3. element
4. fossil fuel
6. contract
7. data
8. expand

Down
1. conservation
2. depletion
5. fossil
9. alloy

page 120

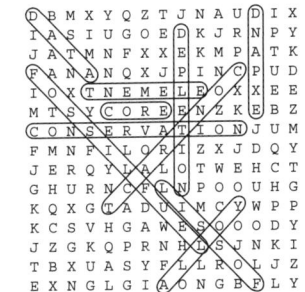

Earth Science 7
(pages 121-126)

page 122
1. elevation
2. Hazardous waste
3. front
4. quasar
5. equator
6. Adaptation
7. hemisphere
8. Condensation
9. conifer
10. conduction

page 123
1. front
2. elevation
3. quasar
4. hazardous waste
5. conifer
6. adaptation
7. equator
8. hemisphere
9. conduction
10. condensation

page 124
Answers will vary.

page 125
Across
3. quasar
7. equator
8. hazardous waste
9. conifer
10. front

Down
1. hemisphere
2. condensation
4. adaptation
5. elevation
6. conduction

page 126

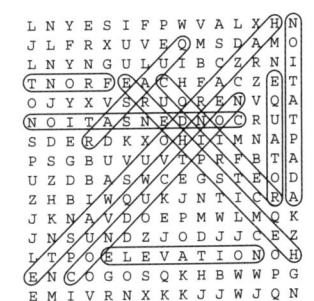

English 1
(pages 127-132)

page 128
1. apostrophe
2. comma
3. capitalize
4. contraction
5. semicolon
6. quotation marks
7. end marks
8. abbreviation
9. colon
10. proofread

page 129
1. contraction
2. apostrophe
3. proofread
4. capitalize
5. end marks
6. colon
7. abbreviation
8. quotation marks
9. comma
10. semicolon

page 130
Answers will vary.

page 131
Across
3. apostrophe
5. proofread
6. quotation marks
7. capitalize
8. colon

Down
1. contraction
2. semicolon
3. abbreviation
4. end marks
7. comma

page 132

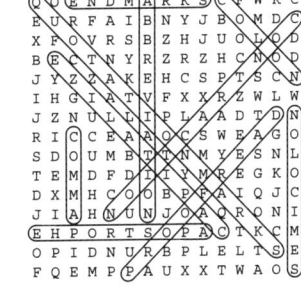

English 2
(pages 133-138)

page 134
1. verb
2. superlative
3. adjective
4. noun
5. simile
6. adverb
7. proper noun
8. comparative
9. pronoun
10. metaphor

page 135
1. simile
2. verb
3. pronoun
4. superlative
5. noun
6. adverb
7. metaphor
8. adjective
9. proper noun
10. comparative

page 136
Answers will vary.

page 137
Across
4. pronoun
6. adjective
7. noun
8. metaphor
9. simile
10. comparative

Down
1. verb
2. superlative
3. adverb
5. proper noun

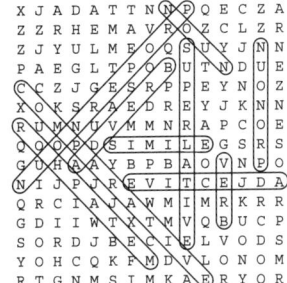

page 138

100% Curriculum Vocabulary—Grades 6-12   281   Copyright © 2002 LinguiSystems, Inc.

Answer Key, continued

English 3
(pages 139-144)

page 140
1. topic
2. main idea
3. context
4. conclusion
5. draft
6. paragraph
7. idea
8. Plagiarism
9. order
10. diagram

page 141
1. context
2. conclusion
3. plagiarism
4. main idea
5. paragraph
6. diagram
7. topic
8. order
9. draft
10. idea

page 142
Answers will vary.

page 143
Across
4. diagram
5. plagiarism
7. draft
9. order
10. idea

Down
1. conclusion
2. paragraph
3. main idea
6. context
8. topic

page 144

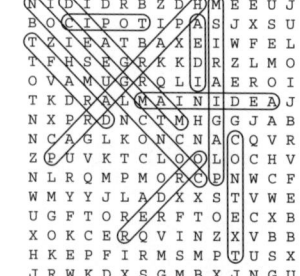

English 4
(pages 145-150)

page 146
1. anonymous
2. Nonfiction
3. plot
4. character
5. analogy
6. anecdote
7. persuasion
8. idiom
9. author
10. myth

page 147
1. myth
2. anecdote
3. character
4. anonymous
5. author
6. nonfiction
7. idiom
8. analogy
9. plot
10. persuasion

page 148
Answers will vary.

page 149
Across
1. plot
4. anecdote
5. analogy
6. idiom
7. nonfiction
8. author

Down
1. persuasion
2. myth
3. character
4. anonymous

page 150

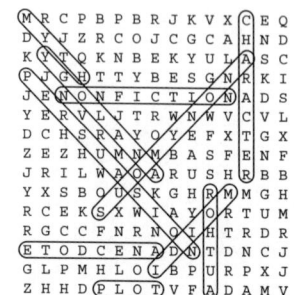

English 5
(pages 151-156)

page 152
1. explanation
2. between
3. except
4. clarify
5. accept
6. opinion
7. fact
8. among
9. mediate
10. instruction

page 153
1. except
2. between
3. fact
4. mediate
5. instruction
6. accept
7. explanation
8. clarify
9. among
10. opinion

page 154
Answers will vary.

page 155
Across
1. fact
5. explanation
6. clarify
7. between
9. opinion
10. accept

Down
2. among
3. mediate
4. instruction
8. except

page 156

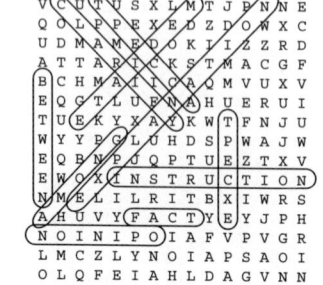

English 6
(pages 157-162)

page 158
1. There
2. their
3. then
4. than
5. your
6. dictionary
7. principal
8. they're
9. principle
10. you're

page 159
1. their
2. you're
3. your
4. than
5. principal
6. principle
7. there
8. they're
9. then
10. dictionary

page 160
Answers will vary.

page 161
Across
1. then
4. principle
8. dictionary

Down
1. they're
2. you're
3. than
5. principal
6. their
7. your
9. there

page 162

Answer Key, continued

English 7
(pages 163-168)

page 164
1. independent clause
2. phrase
3. clause
4. description
5. detail
6. statement
7. dependent clause
8. autobiography
9. double negative
10. encyclopedia

page 165
1. detail
2. independent clause
3. statement
4. clause
5. double negative
6. dependent clause
7. encyclopedia
8. phrase
9. autobiography
10. description

page 166
Answers will vary.

page 167
Across
4. double negative
6. clause
7. autobiography
8. statement
9. independent clause

Down
1. encyclopedia
2. phrase
3. detail
4. dependent clause
5. description

page 168

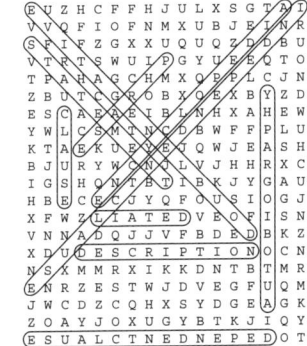

Government 1
(pages 169-174)

page 170
1. boycott
2. deficit
3. document
4. economy
5. excise tax
6. free enterprise
7. loss
8. profit
9. surplus
10. tariff

page 171
1. free enterprise
2. boycott
3. surplus
4. profit
5. deficit
6. economy
7. document
8. loss
9. tariff
10. excise tax

page 172
Answers will vary.

page 173
Across
5. deficit
6. document
8. loss
10. free enterprise

Down
1. tariff
2. profit
3. boycott
4. economy
7. excise tax
9. surplus

page 174

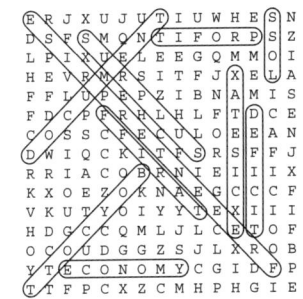

Government 2
(pages 175-180)

page 176
1. veto
2. session
3. judicial system
4. executive branch
5. democracy
6. Congress
7. Senate
8. monarchy
9. consent
10. House of Representatives

page 177
1. veto
2. Congress
3. democracy
4. House of Representatives
5. session
6. judicial system
7. Senate
8. monarchy
9. executive branch
10. consent

page 178
Answers will vary.

page 179
Across
5. executive branch
6. Congress
8. consent
10. judicial system

Down
1. House of Representatives
2. monarchy
3. democracy
4. session
7. Senate
9. veto

page 180

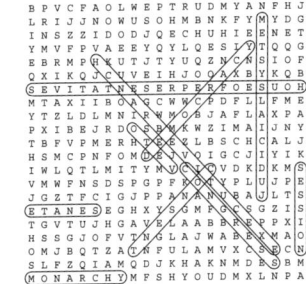

Government 3
(pages 181-186)

page 182
1. acquit
2. immigrant
3. majority
4. minority
5. indict
6. debate
7. candidate
8. voter
9. jury
10. native

page 183
1. jury
2. voter
3. immigrant
4. native
5. minority
6. debate
7. acquit
8. majority
9. indict
10. candidate

page 184
Answers will vary.

page 185
Across
3. immigrant
5. indict
8. acquit
9. native
10. jury

Down
1. candidate
2. minority
4. majority
6. debate
7. voter

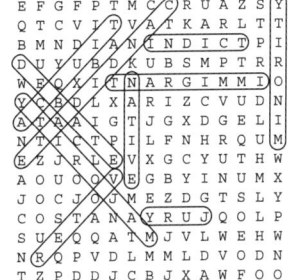

page 186

100% Curriculum Vocabulary—Grades 6-12 283 Copyright © 2002 LinguiSystems, Inc.

Answer Key, continued

Health 1
(pages 187-192)

page 188
1. Displacement
2. extrovert
3. personality
4. introvert
5. body language
6. Abuse
7. Denial
8. emotion
9. neglect
10. risk behavior

page 189
1. emotion
2. displacement
3. body language
4. extrovert
5. neglect
6. risk behavior
7. introvert
8. abuse
9. denial
10. personality

page 190
Answers will vary.

page 191
Across
1. neglect
6. introvert
7. abuse
8. personality
9. extrovert
10. body language

Down
2. emotion
3. risk behavior
4. displacement
5. denial

page 192

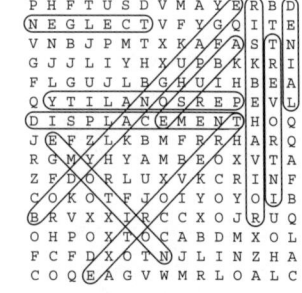

Health 2
(pages 193-198)

page 194
1. ulcer
2. quality of life
3. emphysema
4. Stress
5. stroke
6. High blood pressure
7. wellness
8. homeostasis
9. Sleep apnea
10. Values

page 195
1. ulcer
2. quality of life
3. homeostasis
4. sleep apnea
5. stress
6. values
7. wellness
8. stroke
9. high blood pressure
10. emphysema

page 196
Answers will vary.

page 197
Across
4. quality of life
5. homeostasis
7. sleep apnea
9. wellness
10. stress

Down
1. values
2. stroke
3. high blood pressure
6. emphysema
8. ulcer

page 198

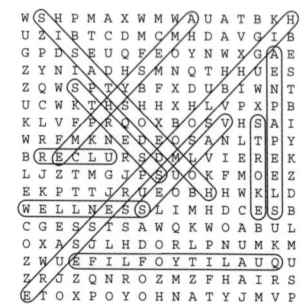

Health 3
(pages 199-204)

page 200
1. immune system
2. physical environment
3. carcinogen
4. Carbohydrates
5. Digestion
6. narcotic
7. Dehydration
8. metabolism
9. habit
10. Adrenaline

page 201
1. habit
2. physical environment
3. carcinogen
4. carbohydrates
5. metabolism
6. immune system
7. adrenaline
8. digestion
9. narcotic
10. dehydration

page 202
Answers will vary.

page 203
Across
3. carcinogen
5. digestion
6. carbohydrates
9. narcotic
10. immune system

Down
1. physical environment
2. metabolism
4. adrenaline
7. habit
8. dehydration

page 204

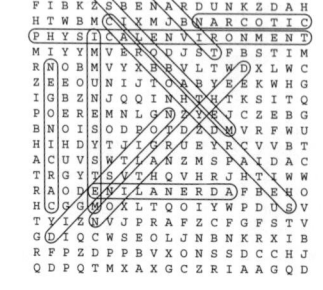

Health 4
(pages 205-210)

page 206
1. vaccination
2. astigmatism
3. diaphragm
4. Eustachian tube
5. plaque
6. Epilepsy
7. Fetal Alcohol Syndrome
8. gingivitis
9. asthma
10. Color blindness

page 207
1. Eustachian tube
2. astigmatism
3. asthma
4. epilepsy
5. vaccination
6. Fetal Alcohol Syndrome
7. diaphragm
8. color blindness
9. gingivitis
10. plaque

page 208
Answers will vary.

page 209
Across
2. asthma
3. plaque
6. vaccination
8. astigmatism
9. gingivitis
10. Fetal Alcohol Syndrome

Down
1. diaphragm
4. epilepsy
5. Eustachian tube
7. color blindness

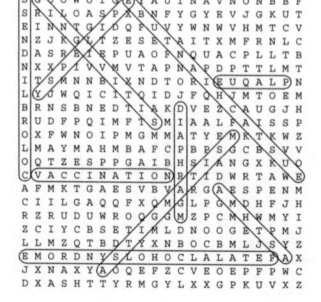

page 210

Answer Key, continued

Health 5
(pages 211-216)

page 212
1. Schizophrenia
2. amnesia
3. phobia
4. anorexia nervosa
5. psychiatrist
6. Obsessive-compulsive disorder
7. Depression
8. Manic-depressive disorder
9. bulimia
10. anxiety disorder

page 213
1. amnesia
2. obsessive-compulsive disorder
3. manic-depressive disorder
4. bulimia
5. phobia
6. anxiety disorder
7. psychiatrist
8. anorexia nervosa
9. depression
10. schizophrenia

page 214
Answers will vary.

page 215
Across
4. anxiety disorder
5. schizophrenia
6. psychiatrist
10. obsessive-compulsive disorder

Down
1. anorexia nervosa
2. manic-depressive disorder
3. depression
7. amnesia
8. bulimia
9. phobia

page 216

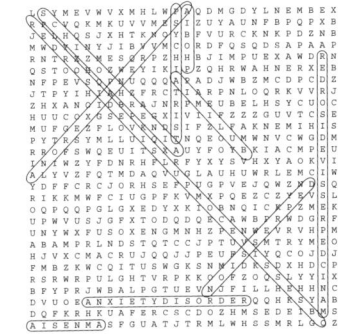

History 1
(pages 217-222)

page 218
1. Indentured servants
2. plantation
3. Union
4. Underground Railroad
5. abolitionist
6. secede
7. Confederacy
8. Carpetbaggers
9. blockade
10. Sharecropping

page 219
1. indentured servants
2. blockade
3. Union
4. abolitionist
5. plantation
6. sharecropping
7. Underground Railroad
8. secede
9. Confederacy
10. carpetbaggers

page 220
Answers will vary.

page 221
Across
1. Union
6. carpetbaggers
8. Confederacy
10. Underground Railroad

Down
2. indentured servants
3. sharecropping
4. secede
5. blockade
7. abolitionist
9. plantation

page 222

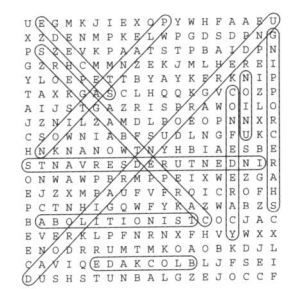

History 2
(pages 223-228)

page 224
1. invasion
2. ration
3. Refugees
4. traitor
5. overthrow
6. anti-Semitism
7. concentration camp
8. dictator
9. emigrate
10. Holocaust

page 225
1. traitor
2. dictator
3. invasion
4. overthrow
5. Holocaust
6. concentration camp
7. emigrate
8. ration
9. refugees
10. anti-Semitism

page 226
Answers will vary.

page 227
Across
3. Holocaust
6. anti-Semitism
7. dictator
8. emigrate
9. refugees
10. ration

Down
1. traitor
2. invasion
4. overthrow
5. concentration camp

page 228

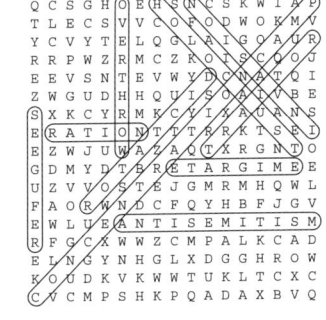

History 3
(pages 229-234)

page 230
1. truce
2. Loyalists
3. forty-niners
4. boycott
5. Dust Bowl
6. depression
7. wagon train
8. Prohibition
9. Expansion
10. Colonies

page 231
1. Prohibition
2. truce
3. depression
4. Dust Bowl
5. boycott
6. wagon train
7. loyalists
8. colonies
9. forty-niners
10. expansion

page 232
Answers will vary.

page 233
Across
2. Prohibition
3. truce
5. wagon train
6. depression
8. loyalists
10. Dust Bowl

Down
1. forty-niners
4. expansion
7. colonies
9. boycott

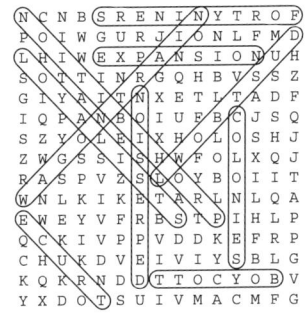

page 234

Answer Key, continued

Keyboarding 1
(pages 235-240)

page 236
1. Tab
2. Enter
3. Caps Lock
4. word processing
5. Shift
6. Backspace
7. Insert
8. Escape
9. keyboard
10. Control

page 237
1. keyboard
2. word processing
3. Escape
4. Enter
5. Tab
6. Control
7. Insert
8. Backspace
9. Caps Lock
10. Shift

page 238
Answers will vary.

page 239
Across
3. keyboard
6. Control
8. Enter
9. Backspace

Down
1. Caps Lock
2. word processing
4. Escape
5. Insert
7. Tab
10. Shift

page 240

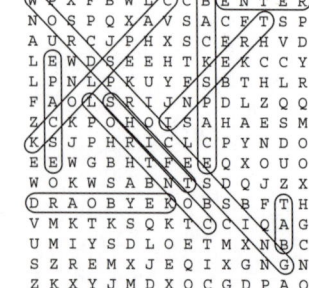

Keyboarding 2
(pages 241-246)

page 242
1. save
2. search
3. indent
4. directory
5. error
6. print
7. accuracy
8. delete
9. retrieve
10. word wrap

page 243
1. indent
2. save
3. error
4. word wrap
5. directory
6. retrieve
7. accuracy
8. print
9. delete
10. search

page 244
Answers will vary.

page 245
Across
3. word wrap
7. retrieve
10. directory

Down
1. search
2. delete
4. accuracy
5. indent
6. save
8. error
9. print

page 246

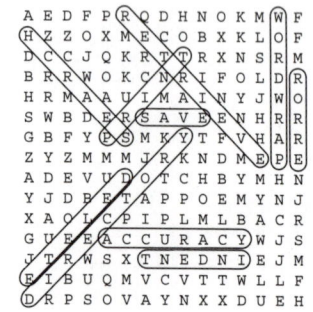

Keyboarding 3
(pages 247-252)

page 248
1. margin
2. backup copy
3. double space
4. single space
5. printer
6. Centering
7. cursor
8. header/footer
9. bold
10. format

page 249
1. double space
2. format
3. single space
4. printer
5. bold
6. cursor
7. backup copy
8. header/footer
9. margin
10. centering

page 250
Answers will vary.

page 251
Across
5. printer
6. bold
7. centering
8. backup copy
9. header/footer

Down
1. double space
2. single space
3. margin
4. cursor
10. format

page 252

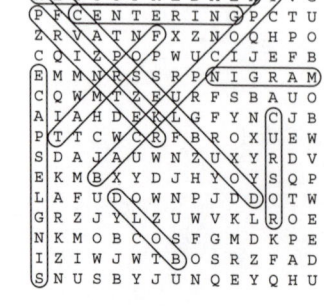

Math 1
(pages 253-258)

page 254
1. circumference
2. angle
3. diameter
4. perimeter
5. congruent
6. Geometry
7. parallel lines
8. bisect
9. tangent
10. arc

page 255
1. circumference
2. geometry
3. angle
4. parallel lines
5. bisect
6. tangent
7. congruent
8. perimeter
9. arc
10. diameter

page 256
Answers will vary.

page 257
Across
2. parallel lines
5. congruent
7. perimeter
9. diameter
10. tangent

Down
1. circumference
3. angle
4. arc
6. geometry
8. bisect

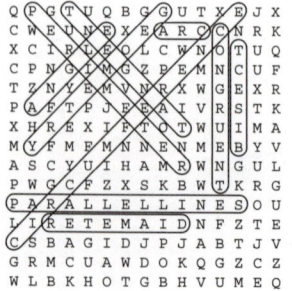

page 258

100% Curriculum Vocabulary—Grades 6-12   286   Copyright © 2002 LinguiSystems, Inc.

Answer Key, continued

Math 2
(pages 259-264)

page 260
1. decrease
2. denominator
3. percent
4. division
5. increase
6. fraction
7. protractor
8. dividend
9. compass
10. numerator

page 261
1. compass
2. denominator
3. fraction
4. protractor
5. decrease
6. dividend
7. division
8. increase
9. numerator
10. percent

page 262
Answers will vary.

page 263
Across
3. compass
4. percent
7. numerator
8. decrease
9. fraction
10. denominator

Down
1. increase
2. dividend
5. protractor
6. division

page 264

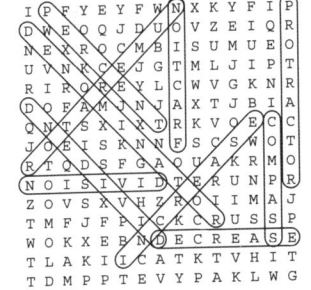

Math 3
(pages 265-270)

page 266
1. coordinates
2. even number
3. algebra
4. line graph
5. negative number
6. equation
7. bar graph
8. integer
9. decimal
10. Addition

page 267
1. even number
2. line graph
3. integer
4. addition
5. coordinates
6. equation
7. bar graph
8. decimal
9. negative number
10. algebra

page 268
Answers will vary.

page 269
Across
1. coordinates
4. decimal
7. addition
9. equation
10. line graph

Down
2. negative number
3. even number
5. integer
6. bar graph
8. algebra

page 270

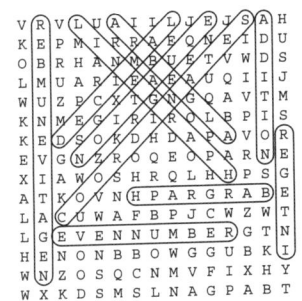

Math 4
(pages 271-276)

page 272
1. solution
2. foot
3. review
4. inch
5. Volume
6. pound
7. length
8. yard
9. gallon
10. quart

page 273
1. review
2. foot
3. gallon
4. yard
5. solution
6. quart
7. pound
8. volume
9. inch
10. length

page 274
Answers will vary.

page 275
Across
5. volume
6. yard
7. length
9. solution

Down
1. foot
2. pound
3. review
4. quart
8. gallon
10. inch

page 276

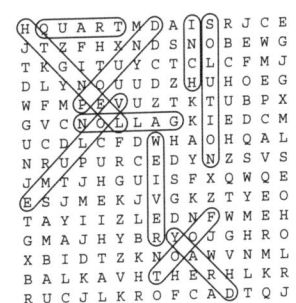

100% Curriculum Vocabulary—Grades 6-12   287   Copyright © 2002 LinguiSystems, Inc.

21-05-987654